GW00702453

Years of Horror—
Glimpse of Hope

Years of Horror— Glimpse of Hope

The Diary of a Family in Hiding

by
Moshe Maltz

Translated from the Yiddish and adapted by
Gertrude Hirschler

SHENGOLD PUBLISHERS, INC.
New York

Library of Congress Catalog Card Number: 93-086349
ISBN 0-88400-168-7
Copyright © 1993 by Herbert Maltz
All rights reserved

Published by Shengold Publishers, Inc.
18 West 45th Street
New York, NY 10036

Printed in the United States of America

Dedicated to our beloved uncle
Sam (Shmelke) Maltz,
the brother of the author, whose courage not only enabled us to
survive the years of horror, but has been a constant source of
hope and inspiration.

*Left: Interior of the Sokal
Synagogue.*

*Below: The Main synagogue
of Sokal.*

Introduction

I shall not die but live and recount the deeds of the Lord.
(Psalms 118:17)

We deeply regret the fact that our father, Moshe Maltz, did not live to see this book become a reality. For 50 years this diary, which he kept in Yiddish during those years of horror, was waiting to see the light of day. By then we had undertaken the task of having the diary translated into English. Then, during the final stages of publication, our beloved mother passed away, on September 3, 1993. May their souls rest among the holy and righteous who shine bright in the firmament.

Now that our children can no longer listen to their grandfather tell his personal recollections, we realize the importance of having a permanent record of those tragic times, for our children, grandchildren, and all future generations.

Special mention must be made of our dear uncle, Sam (Shmelke) Maltz, for without him our family certainly would not have survived. He risked his life many times to save family members, and because of his heroic efforts we are here today.

Our father did not only wish to memorialize the holy Jewish community of Sokal which is no more, but also to let the world know how German brutality put an end to so many innocent lives and removed from this world a centuries-old vibrant community of men, women and children. It is our sincere hope that by publishing this book the memory of the martyred Jewish community of Sokal will live on, and the world will have some further proof that the unthinkable can happen when innocent, defenseless people are at the mercy of brutal regimes like the one that existed in Germany only 50 years ago.

Herbert and Nathan Maltz

Never say that there is only death for you,
Though leaden skies may be concealing days of blue—
Because the hour we have hungered for is near:
Beneath our tread the earth shall tremble: We are here!

Jewish Partisan Song, by Hirsch Glick; translated from the
Yiddish by Aaron Kramer, quoted in Jacob Gladstein, Israel
Knox, Samuel Margoshes, et al., eds., *Anthology of
Holocaust Literature*, Philadelphia, The Jewish Publication
Society of America, 1968.

Left: The author's grandfather, Meyer Zvi, 1939.
Right: Joseph Maltz, the author's father.

I

Sokal

Sokal, Autumn, 1939

The world's second big war in 25 years has begun. Germany and the Soviet Union have divided Poland between themselves.

My family and I lived in Sokal, a town in East Galicia. The River Bug, which flows through Sokal, has become the boundary line between the German and Soviet sectors of Poland. My home and the home of my parents are east of the river, in the Soviet sector. The railroad station is now in German hands; so is the town of Krystynopol, ten kilometers from Sokal, where I was born on May 17, 1902.

My name is Moshe Maltz. I am 37 years old. My wife, Chana, is 30. We have been married five years and have one son, Chaim, who is three.

• • •

Jewish refugees from the German-occupied sector, west of the River Bug, are streaming into out part of town which, as I have said, is now under Soviet occupation* Our Jewish families have opened their homes to the refugees. Temporary shelters have been set up also in the synagogue and *batei midrashim*,** and a soup kitchen has been organized.

The Soviet sector of Sokal is run by a gang of Communists and Communist fellow travelers, Gentile and Jewish. Underworld characters who have been serving prison terms for theft and other offenses claim they were imprisoned only because they were Communists; they have been released by the Soviet occupation authorities and have become big shots and informers.

---

* In 1921, after Sokal had become part of the Poland Republic, its Jewish population was 4,360, or 43 percent of the total population. When World War II broke out, the Jewish refugees from the Nazi-occupied sector of Poland swelled the number to over 6,000.

** "Houses of study." Rooms or halls where groups of Jews gather for study and worship. The setting is usually less formal than that of a synagogue.

Private enterprise has been declared illegal in the Soviet sector. Ten Jews have been arrested for engaging in private business; they have been sent to labor camps deep inside Russia for terms of seven to ten years.

A committee of Ukrainian peasants,* including individuals who have been employed with our family for 20 years and more, has informed my father that our family business and all our other assets are now the property of the Soviet state.

My father, Joseph Maltz, is a cattle dealer. Before the war, we exported cattle to Czechoslovakia and as far away as Italy. We also owned a small hotel and a house in town, and some farmland on the outskirts. Now the Soviets have confiscated everything—our cattle and horses, our farm tools and even our radios. They have also taken our hotel. They ordered us to hand over the keys to the guest rooms (all 16 of them) and that was that. My father and my mother, Rivka, are facing old age as paupers.

Zolkiew, Summer, 1940

Most of the Jewish refugees from the Nazi-occupied sector of Poland have been deported to Siberia as security risks because they refused to accept Soviet citizenship. All other Jews have been ordered to leave Sokal and move further inland into Soviet-held territory, at least 50 kilometers east of the border. The explanation given us is that, living so close to the German sector, just across the River Bug, the Jews whose property has been confiscated by the Soviets might take revenge and become spies for Hitler's Germany!

Among the Jewish refugees expelled from Sokal was the Hasidic Rebbe of Belz, Rabbi Aaron Rokeach,** of blessed memory. Thanks to someone's personal intervention with the NKVD, the Soviet secret

---

* The Gentile population of Sokal consisted of Ukrainians and Poles. In the mutual hatred between the Ukrainian and Polish ethnic groups, the Jews were usually caught in the middle.

** Rabbi Rokeach (1880–1957) had fled to Sokal when the Nazis occupied Belz. He eventually went to Przemsyl, where 33 members of his family perished at the hands of the Nazis. After confinement to various Polish ghettos, the Rebbe was deported to Košice, Slovakia, and finally made his way to Budapest, where he was liberated by Soviet troops. After the war, he settled in Israel.

police, the rebbe and his family were permitted to remain in Sokal until after the festival of Shevuoth, which fell early in June this year.

Most of the "old timers" like ourselves who were merely expelled—not deported—from Sokal have gone to places where they already have family or friends. We chose Zolkiew, about 50 kilometers east of Sokal, mainly because my wife's parents, the Holtzmans, are living there.

On July 3, 1940 we left Sokal for Zolkiew. The journey took us three days; we had to travel on foot all the way because our railroad station is in German territory. There were eight of us: Chana and I and our little boy; my parents (Mother in her late fifties, Father past sixty); my two unmarried younger sisters, Yitte, 32, and Chaye Dvora, 27; and my only brother, Shmelke, who at 25 is still single and, like Yitte and Chaye Dvora, has been living at home with our parents.

For the first two weeks in Zolkiew, all of us—three men, four women and one child—camped in the stable of a friend, the cattle dealer, Chaim Friedman. Then we moved into a damp, miserable apartment of our own. Because our Soviet papers state that we are "capitalists," former members of the propertied class, we cannot get jobs. So we have been living partly on the generosity of Chana's parents, who still have some money, and partly from "occasional" business transactions that seem to be flourishing in Zolkiew despite the Russians.

My oldest sister, Leah, 34, and her husband, Eli Letzter, and their baby daughter, Feyge Chashe, have been permitted to remain in Sokal thus far because Eli never owned enough property to be classified as a "capitalist."

Lea and Eli Letzter, 1938, Sokal. The author's sister and her husband.

II

Zolkiew

Germany and the Soviet Union, those two former allies, are now at war with one another. Zolkiew's population is in a state of panic. The Ukrainians, who pretended loyalty to the Soviet Union as long as the Russians occupied the city, are showing their true colors now. The Ukrainians hate the Russians, the Communists, the Poles and the Jews (although not necessarily in that order). Ukrainian snipers are taking potshots at the Russians, who are desperately trying to repel the German invaders. The Russians shoot back. A number of Jews have already been killed in the crossfire. Jews don't dare to venture outside.

• • •

On June 29th, a week after the outbreak of war between Russia and Germany, the Germans occupy Zolkiew. German troops are shelling the ancient, historic synagogue of Zolkiew, which was built in the 1600s by special permission from Poland's King Jan Sobieski. The synagogue burns for three days—with dozens of Jews inside—until nothing is left but rubble and ashes.

The peasants of Zolkiew and the surrounding areas have taken over the stores owned by Jews who have been killed. The Germans have informed them that all surviving Jews will be assembled for "selection"; this means that they, the peasants, will be allowed to "select" any Jews they want for slave labor on their farms.

The Germans have set up a *Judenrat* * in Zolkiew. This puppet

---

* Literally, "Jew Council." The Title *Jüdischer Rat* (Jewish Council) apparently seemed too respectable to the Nazis. *Judenrat* were appointed by the German authorities in most Nazi-occupied Jewish communities to carry out Nazi orders. The *Judenrat* were forced to supply Jewish slave laborers and often to draw up lists of Jews for deportation. Whether various *Judenrat* members could have taken effective action to save their fellow Jews, or whether some of them collaborated with the Nazis under the Naive illusion that this would save their own lives and the lives of their families,

community council has issued orders that all Jews, male and female, between the ages of 14 and 60, are to report at headquarters of the *Judenrat* each morning for assignment to various labor details. There are rumors that some of these Jews are killed while they work. The killing is done by Poles of Ukrainian nationality.

On the second Sunday following the Nazi occupation of Zolkiew, Ukrainians from surrounding villages appear in town. They seize Jews and beat them up. The Jews are going into hiding. Some neighbors and my family take shelter in an attic. We can hear the cries and moans of Jews outside, mingled with the barking of dogs. This continues until one o'clock the next morning. The Germans, who are supposed to be preserving law and order in Zolkiew, are under the command of a Slovak officer.* The *Judenrat* of Zolkiew has assigned the most unpleasant menial tasks to Jews from out of town.

We are living under unspeakable conditions. There is no food. My father has developed all kinds of ailments. Also, there has been an addition to our family. In August, my wife gave birth to our second child, a little girl, whom we have named Lifshe.

The Soviet sector of Sokal, our home town, was occupied by the Germans almost immediately upon the outbreak of the fighting. German troops crossed the River Bug, meeting virtually no resistance. So both Zolkiew and all of Sokal are in the hands of the Nazis now. Still, we hear that life is a little easier in Sokal than in Zolkiew. With the Communists gone, we might even find a way of reclaiming some property—of nothing else but our homes. We should be able to outlast the Germans. Living in our home town will give us a better chance of survival than continuing to subsist as fugitives in Zolkiew, with our sick father and our month-old baby daughter. Jews are forbidden to travel, but I am willing to take the risk. I know that we will not be able to survive much longer in Zolkiew.

---

has been a subject of acrimonious debate to this day. Some defend members of the *Judenrat* as heroes and martyrs; others condemn them as cowards and traitors.

* Slovakia, long known for its strong anti-Semitic tendencies, became a Nazi puppet state on March 14, 1939, the day before the Germans occupied Bohemia and Moravia. After the war, Nazi Slovakia's make-believe ruler, Josef Tiso, a Catholic priest, was tried and executed as a war criminal.

On the road, Autumn, 1941

On September 25, two days after Rosh HaShana, we hire a horse and wagon and leave Zolkiew for Sokal. Near the town limits of Zolkiew, a mean-looking character rides up to us on his bicycle and orders us to get off the wagon. "You Jews aren't sick," he says. "You should be walking and not make that poor horse work so hard." I don't want any trouble, so we climb down from the wagon and start walking, with Chana carrying our baby Lifshe. The wagon follows us slowly, at some distance, with our baggage.

After a march of two or three kilometers, we arrive at the village of Torinka. Ukrainian policemen, who are now working for the Germans, stop us and search our wagon. I don't like this; Torinka is known as the most anti-Semitic village in the district. Only a week ago, we are told, the Ukrainians took five Jews from Torinka into the woods nearby and shot them.

The Ukrainian policemen question us for several hours. Why are we traveling and where are we going? When I have run out of explanations, I finally tell them that we were driven from our homes by the Russians (whom the Ukrainians, of course, consider their worst enemies) and want to go home again. I even produce a Soviet document from Sokal stating that our assets were "nationalized" by the Red Army. This does the trick. The Ukrainians take pity on us, the victims of the Bolsheviks, and allow us to proceed. They even permit us to climb back onto our wagon.

We travel until we reach the town of Mosty Wielkie. There we climb down from our wagon once again and walk some distance ahead because the wagon driver says he's afraid he'll get into trouble with the Ukrainians if they see him driving a wagonload of Jews.

In Mosty Wielkie we pass the burned-out shell of what was once the town's synagogue. We hear that several weeks earlier, the Germans locked 21 Jews into this synagogue and set fire to them along with the building.

Leaving Mosty Wielkie, we climb back onto our wagon and continue on our way to Sokal. In the evening we arrive at Parchatz, about a dozen kilometers from Mosty Wielkie. A few Jews are still left there; they seem depressed and apprehensive. They do not know what the next day will bring, but one family, that of Eli Porchetzer, a very good friend of my father's, gives us a hot meal and some clothes.

We leave Parchatz before dawn the next day. On each side of the highway there are bullet-ridden tanks lying on their sides, burned-out army trucks and graves with makeshift markers topped by German army helmets.

At one o'clock that afternoon, we reach the town of Protozice. On the outskirts of the town, two Ukrainian policemen stop us. "Who gave you permission to travel?" they want to know. It turns out that they are from Sokal. I tell them that we are the Maltzes, that we were expelled from Sokal and our property was nationalized by the Soviets. Now, with the Soviet gone, we want to go home. Again, my story works. "So you're the Maltzes from Sokal? You may proceed. But you better get off the main highway and use the side roads so the Germans don't see you," the older of the two Ukrainians says.

Dvora Maltz (top row, second from left), the sister of Moshe.

III

Sokal Under Nazis

We are back home in Sokal after an absence of 15 months. The following is a report of what happened here, in our home town, since the beginning of the Soviet–German war this summer.

The Germans captured all of Sokal on June 22, 1941, less than an hour after fighting broke out between the armies of Hitler and Stalin. The Ukrainian population, who had pretended to be staunch Communists under the Soviets, welcomed the columns of Nazi tanks with bouquets of flowers and shouts of "Heil Hitler!" As a reward for their cooperation, the Ukrainian turncoats who had run the town under the Russians were allowed to keep their jobs under the Germans.

A Ukrainian by the name of Chernetsky was appointed mayor of Sokal and immediately organized a Ukrainian militia to carry out the orders of the Germans. On June 30, all Jewish males between the ages of 14 and 60 were ordered to report at the *targevicze*, the open square where cattle were assembled and sold.

Chana's sister, Leah and brother-in-law on the 1930s,
killed with their three daughters.

When the Jews arrived at the *targevicze,* a crowd of Ukrainians was already there, waiting for them, dressed in their Sunday best as if they had all been invited to a party. Some big shots took over and announced that 400 Jewish males were required for labor assignments. They then proceeded to select 400—professionals, businessmen, workers and ordinary able-bodied individuals, all at random—and turned them over to a detachment of SS men. Among the 400 "selectees" was Eli Letzter, my sister Leah's husband.

The 400 were marched off to a brick factory just outside Sokal. There they were shot and their bodies tossed into a mass grave. That is how my sister lost her husband, and my baby niece Feyge Chashe, her father. Some parents lost two, three and even four sons in this massacre.

Many of the surviving parents, wives and children cannot bring themselves to accept the truth. They try to persuade themselves that their men have been "resettled" in a labor camp to work for the Germans. They have even made a collection of money so they will be able to send food and clothing to their husbands, sons and brothers as soon as they have direct news from them. Wives are traveling all over the countryside, questioning other Jews and also Gentiles for news, any news, of the 400 men who were rounded up in Sokal. There are Gentiles who exploit the naiveté of the Jewish women. They tell them that the men have indeed been taken to a labor camp. Just where, they are not sure, but they may be able to find out if the women will pay them for the work and expense involved. I know of women who actually fell for this line and paid Gentiles good money in hopes of receiving good news which will never come.

What fools we were to think that if we returned to Sokal we would get our property back! We found our old homes again, intact, but that is all. Ukrainians from the countryside are pouring into Sokal and other Nazi-occupied cities are seizing all Jewish-owned stores and businesses. The former owners, the unfortunate Jews, must watch without a word of protest while the Ukrainians

Chana's brother, Mordechai in the 1930s. He was among the first Jews killed in 1941.

decorate the windows of their stores with pictures of Hitler and vile cartoons depicting Jews as bloodsucking parasites.

• • •

The Germans have set up a *Judenrat* in Sokal, consisting of a chairman and seven board members, assisted by an office staff and a Jewish police force. The *Judenrat* announces and enforces the orders of the Germans.

Every Jewish person from the age of ten must wear a white armband with a blue Star of David sewn to his or her right sleeve so that the Germans should not, heaven forbid, mistake a Jew for a human being. All Jewish males must have their heads close-shaven; they are not allowed to wear hats or any other headgear. Jews are forbidden to travel out of town. Any Jew caught buying eggs, butter or milk from a Gentile is subject to the death penalty. All Jew, male and female, between the ages of 14 and 60 must assemble at seven o'clock each morning in front of the building assigned as headquarters for the *Judenrat.* Germans and Ukrainians—factory owners, storekeepers, farmers— are entitled to come there and select as many Jews as they want to work for them. They simply walk into the *Judenrat* building and tell the Jewish *Arbeitsamt* (labor office), "I want 20 Jews to work in my factory," or "I need ten Jews to work in my store."

One hundred Jews have been assigned to work for the Sokal department of police and sanitation as street cleaners. By four o'clock each morning, these Jews are out sweeping the streets, regardless of whether or not the streets need cleaning at that early hour. The Jewish street cleaners, mostly elderly men with their heads bare, their beards shaven off and with long brooms in their hands, are a pitiful sight. Gentiles who walk or drive past them jeer and laugh; apparently they enjoy seeing these old Jews in their misery and humiliation.

The office staff of the *Judenrat,* assisted by the Jewish police, conducts searches of Jewish homes for well-made, elegant furniture and other household goods. These articles are confiscated and taken to a warehouse set up by the *Judenrat* for this purpose. They are kept there for use as gifts to appease the German and Ukrainian officials as the need arises.

Most of the Jews who lived in Sokal before the war and—like ourselves—were expelled by the Soviets are now returning. Jews from nearby towns and villages who have relatives in Sokal are also moving here. It is really true; the Jews here in Sokal are better off than those in many other Polish localities occupied by the Nazis. We still have some food while the Jews in many of the other places are starving.

All Jews who wish to settle in Sokal, or who are returning here, must register immediately with the *Judenrat* and pay the tax which the *Judenrat* collects from all Jewish householders. The money is needed, we are told, for cash bribes to Ukrainian officials and German Gestapo men. (Sokal is the Gestapo center for the entire surrounding district.) The money is used also for furnishing the homes of the high-ranking Ukrainian and German authorities who cannot be expected to make due with second-hand furniture obtained from Jews. The Provincial Commissioner and the top Gestapo officers in this district, for instance, must have custom-made furniture from Lvov. This costs a lot of money and the Jews are expected to pay for it.

The *Judenrat* officially assesses the tax to be paid by each Jewish householder. If a Jew fails, or refuses, to pay, then the Jewish police, acting on orders of the *Judenrat*, raids his home and confiscates valuables in lieu of the tax. Some Jews have been arrested by the Jewish police for non-payment of taxes. They are locked up in one of the two small detention rooms set aside as a sort of prison at *Judenrat* police for non-payment of taxes, and they remain there until their taxes are paid—either by themselves or perhaps by a more fortunate friend willing to bail them out.

Sokal, November, 1941

Until recently, Jews were assigned by the *Judenrat* to work for any Gentile who said he needed workers. No special papers or documents were necessary. But now the Germans have changed that rule. All Jewish males between the ages of 16 and 45, must have *Meldekarten* (registration cards). Each *Meldekarte* must have a photograph of the holder and must be signed by the Gentile for whom the holder is working. A Jew without a *Meldekarte* or without an employer to sign the card can be picked up on the street by the Germans or Ukrainians and will be taken straight to a labor camp.

So the Jews of Sokal are frantic; those with no Gentile employer are contacting Gentile acquaintances, begging them to give them jobs, or at least to sign for then as their employers.

Gentiles are hiring Jewish women as cooks and maids for slave labor wages. Girls from the most prominent Jewish families in town are now maids of Gentiles who were virtually paupers before the war.

My own sister, Chaye Dvora, is working as a maid for a Ukrainian family.

In addition to showing proof of "legitimate" employment, all able-bodied Jews must register with the German *Arbeitsamt*, which is staffed by Ukrainians and is not identical with the *Arbeitsamt*, or labor office, of the *Judenrat*. They must report to this German office again every week thereafter to have their *Meldekarte* stamped.

I stand in line along with the rest of the Jews in front of the German *Arbeitsamt*. I see bodies swollen from hunger and cold, and children no more than 14 years old bent with pain. There is little Yaakov, the son of Yossel the sexton. Each Friday night at the synagogue, Yossel proudly sang out the names of congregants who would receive honors at the next day's services; now his son is standing in line just ahead of me, in front of the *Arbeitsamt*, looking as if he were bearing all the misery of the Jewish people on his shoulders. The Ukrainian officials just sit there, behind their desks, laughing at the Jews.

Certain privileged characters with special connections do not need a Gentile employer to "legitimize" them. They have managed to get jobs working for the *Judenrat*. (I have a Gentile acquaintance, a cattle dealer and wholesale butcher by the name of Stanislaw Zulchinski, who signs for me as my employer. Actually, I make ends meet by selling our family's belongings and by occasional barter deals.)

I happen to be present at *Judenrat* headquarters while a meeting is going on. This meeting has been called for the more affluent women in the Jewish community. Meir Shafransky, vice-chairman of the *Judenrat*, and one of his associates, Wolf Ertag, announce that the Germans have ordered the Jews of Sokal to supply them with leather, textiles and furniture. When the women hear the amount of money involved, some of them become hysterical and faint.

The *Judenrat* has launched a drive to raise the money. Every Jewish householder is told how much he must contribute. If he refuses, the *Judenrat* expropriates the cash or its equivalent in personal property. This is in addition to the "regular" tax collected by the *Judenrat*.

Sokal, December, 1941

The Germans are paying regular visits to *Judenrat* headquarters to make sure everything is *in Ordnung* (in good order), to check the uniforms of the Jewish police and to inspect the warehouse where their "gifts" are stored.

The other day, a Gestapo bigwig by the name of Hartmann, accompanied by a huge dog, appeared at *Judenrat* headquarters. Joseph Pellenberg, one of the *Judenrat* workers who could speak German, welcomed the visitor and offered to take him wherever he wanted to go. Hartmann announced that he wanted to inspect the warehouse. Meir Linsker, the supervisor of the warehouse, offered him some towels as a gift for Gestapo headquarters. Hartmann didn't like the towels, so Linsker was sent to the Janow Street prison in Lvov where he was tortured until he mercifully died. Poor fellow; he got his job at the warehouse through some special connections. He thought that working for the *Judenrat* would be easy and safe. . . .

Hitler has declared war on the United States. Since then, the persecution of Jews has become more intense. On the morning of December 27, a Sabbath, the *Judenrat* receives orders from the Germans that Jews must turn in all their fur coats, fur hats, fur collars, winter gloves and other articles of warm clothing for shipment to German troops fighting on the Russian battle front. Several prominent Jews have been taken as hostages to make sure the "winter clothing campaign" will be a success. If the "campaign" does not yield the desired results, these hostages will be shot.

On that Sabbath—the temperature is 30 degrees below freezing—the Jews of Sokal deliver their furs and other warm winter clothing to the Germans. This leaves most of our Jews with just their light spring and summer clothes to get through the winter. I also turn in my family's furs, but only the less valuable ones. We pack our really good furs into a couple of milk cans with some mothballs and bury them in the garden of Shmuel Letzter, father of my sister Leah's late husband, Eli Letzter.

The Jews in Sokal are suffering from cold and starvation. Until now the daily bread ration was 33 decagrams (a little less than 12 ounces) for Gentiles and 14 (just under five ounces) for

Lea and Yitta, 1965.

Jews. From now on, Jews will receive only three decagrams (about one ounce) of bread per day. Other foods have become rarities, as good as non-existent in Sokal.

A committee of our Jews has raised money for a soup kitchen, which has been set up at the home of Hersh Daks, a fairly spacious house. The men in charge are Berl Singer and the engineer Schwartz, who has played an active role in our Jewish community, particularly in the Zionist movement, for many years. Jews who had plenty of money before the war, line up each day at the soup kitchen for a bowl of soup. There are Gentiles who, out of simple pity for the Jews, have been secretly sending groceries to the soup kitchen. Heaven help them if the Germans ever find out.

Germans have also been giving Jews wheat in exchange for their old clothes and furniture. The Jews have put together a primitive sort of mill for grinding the wheat. They have even found a way of producing fine flour. The crude flour is used as a thickener for soups; the fine flour makes cookies that are not too bad.

Firewood is unobtainable. The Jews are particularly hard hit by the cold because they have had to give their winter clothes to the Germans.

Meanwhile, the Gestapo is killing Jews. Jewish informers reported to the Gestapo that the son of Hirsh Bild, a plain, ordinary Jew, was actually a very rich man. So the Gestapo arrested his wife. The Bilds sent a woman to the Gestapo prison with food for Mrs. Bild. A Gestapo man caught the woman trying to smuggle the food into the prison through a window. He ordered the woman shot and sent word to the *Judenrat* to have her body removed within 15 minutes.

Nachum Reyer, a lad of 15, who was working at Gestapo headquarters as an errand boy, was sent by the Gestapo cook to buy a kilogram of pork from Stanislaw Zulchinsky, the cattle dealer. The Gestapo woman took the meat for herself. When her superiors discovered the theft, they vented their anger at Nachum; they dragged him off to a place outside town and shot him.

Sokal, February, 1942

On February 24, five Jews from Sokal were taken to a place somewhere on the outskirts of town and shot. One of them was Yeshaye, son of Yankel the coachman. In 1940, during the period of Soviet occupation, Yeshaye had been a coachman working for the NKVD. Now the Gestapo called him and ordered him to turn over to them the reins of his horses. They said to him, "We'll give you three days to deliver those reins to us. If we don't get them by that time, we'll have you shot." Yeshaye thought that the Gestapo must be joking. How could he go on working as a coachman without his reins? Unfortunately for Yeshaye, the Gestapo men were in dead earnest.

Also among the five shot was Dr. Knopf, a lawyer who had converted to Christianity. The Germans had ordered him to dismiss his Gentile maid so that she could be sent to work in Germany. Knopf petitioned the Gestapo to let him have his maid back. That's why the Germans shot him. Despite his baptism, he was simply not an Aryan. The third victim was blind Yankel, who was found guilty of buying and slaughtering a calf. Under German occupation regulations, cattle can be slaughtered only by officially approved butchers.

• • •

There are rumors that Jewish teenage boys will be taken to labor camps in the Zloczow district, about 150 miles from Sokal. These are true death camps. A Jew who arrives there in good health can expect to survive for about ten weeks, if he is lucky. Those with less stamina are likely to die within two weeks. No wonder the Jews of Sokal with teenage sons are in a state of high alarm.

On Friday evening, February 27, four trucks filled with German and Ukrainian police pull up outside the pharmacy. The rumor quickly spreads that Jews will be rounded up during the night, piled onto these trucks and taken to the labor camps. The rumor turns out to be true. The police go to the *Judenrat* headquarters and announce that 500 Jews are needed for labor assignments. Probably no more than 200 are actually needed, but the idea is to squeeze the *Judenrat* a little. In return for "gifts" of leather, textiles, whiskey and cigarettes, the police obligingly agree to make due with 200 Jews instead of 500.

• • •

The *Judenrat* sends out Jewish police, accompanied by Ukrainians, to the town of Tatrakow, nine kilometers from Sokal, to pick up 50 Jewish teenage boys for labor service. Additional boys are rounded up from other localities, chiefly Sokal. All night long, Jewish and Ukrainian policemen march from one house to the next, dragging Jewish boys from their beds and taking them to *Judenrat* headquarters, from where they will be transported to the labor camps. When they can't find teenage boys, the policemen take the father of the family (or, in some cases, even the mother or a young sister) instead.

Sokal, March, 1942

By Saturday, February 28, the news of the previous night's roundup had spread to the neighboring villages. Jews from all these places came to the "assembly point" from which the boys were to leave, bringing food packages for the boys to take with them. The Ukrainians didn't like it and used their whips on every Jew in sight. Some of the boys were sent home and their parents taken in their place.

I looked out through a crack in the wall of my apartment and watched the trucks with the boys pass by. The parents of the boys walked slowly behind the trucks; it looked like a funeral procession. The Ukrainian policemen in the trucks whipped the boys and ordered them to sing something. So the boys sang *HaTikvah,* the Zionist anthem, but the tune to which they sang the words was the age-old chant of Jeremiah's Book of Lamentations.

The camp to which the boys were taken was sheer hell. A hundred bodies were packed into one small barrack with three tiers of bunks in the bitter cold, without any heat. Twice a day the inmates received a little black coffee and a bowl of watery soup with a crust of black bread. They were put to work shoveling the deep snow from the highways near the camp. Each morning, at roll call, they were beaten by their Ukrainian taskmasters. Anyone too weak to report for work was shot then and there. Sometimes a boy was handed a gun and ordered to shoot a fellow inmate who was obviously unfit for work. An inmate who refused to obey such an order was shot together with his friend. Ukrainians used inmates as targets for marksmanship practice.

Epidemics swept through the camp. I heard of one typhoid patient who had to share a bed with two other young men. One of them had TB; the other, an infectious skin disease. Most of the inmates were afraid to report sick for fear of being shot. For every inmate who attempted to escape, ten others were gunned down. The parents and siblings of one Jewish boy who had actually escaped were arrested at their home and brought to the camp, where they were hanged. The bodies were left hanging at the execution site for several days as an object lesson.

• • •

There are rumors each day that additional Jews will be rounded up the next night and transported to a labor camp. So all the Jews of Sokal, young and old, live in hiding all day and in fear all through the night.

During the night of March 10th, the Nazi and Ukrainian gangsters returned to round up additional Jewish boys for the labor camps. This time the *Judenrat* has prepared a cash bribe. The bribe is accepted and no Jews are picked up that night. But in Zolkiew, 40 Jews who were put to work cleaning the streets, were taken away. Among them was my brother-in-law, Leib Holtzman, who lived in Zolkiew. "Dante's *Inferno* is nothing compared to where I am now," Leib wrote in one of his letters to us.

The boys at the labor camp are writing pitiful letters to their families at home. It must be said to the credit of the *Judenrat* that it has been doing a lot for the labor camp inmates. Every Jew in Sokal has to pay the *Judenrat* a new tax, officially known as the "employment tax." The *Judenrat* uses this money to hire cars from the Ukrainians to transport food to the camps. A food transport is sent off every two weeks, accompanied by the religious Zionist leader and Talmudic scholar, Dr. Falik, a gynecologist who is working for the *Judenrat.* Bread and sugar rations allotted to the Jews of Sokal are also sent to the camps, not as food for the inmates, but as bribes for the German and Ukrainian overseers. As a result, the inmates from Sokal receive better treatment, we are told, than those from other localities. Each time Dr. Falik returns from a visit to a labor camp, he reassures the parents of the young inmates that their sons are not too badly off. But he tells me the truth in private; it sends chills through my bones.

• • •

We hear that Jews in Zolkiew and Lvov are being rounded up and transported to an unknown destination. Some 600 Jews have been rounded up in Zolkiew alone; among them are a number of my own relatives and friends. We receive letters from people in Zolkiew and Lvov asking us whether we know anything about the fate of the deportees. They have heard rumors that the deportees have been taken to Polesie, which is not far from Sokal; that is why they think we may know more.

• • •

The Jews of Zolkiew and Lvov will not be left in ignorance much longer. Polish Gentiles working at the railroad station have already told us about a gas chamber that has been built in Belzec, about 65 kilometers from Sokal. There, we hear, Jews are gassed to death and their bodies are cremated. Railroad workers from Polesie have told their friends at the Sokal station that they have seen five to ten trainloads of Jews passing through Polesie each day, bound for Belzec.

Incidentally, my brother Shmelke was in Belzec during the period of Soviet occupation, with a group drafted by the Russians to dig trenches. By a lucky coincidence, Shmelke left Belzec on leave only hours before the Nazi onslaught. Others in his group were not so fortunate.

Sokal, April, 1942

And so the days and nights drag on, with the terror of Belzec added to the fear of starvation. Food is getting scarcer and costlier all the time. Now and then a Jew is killed or beaten up at work, and every two weeks the *Judenrat* still sends shipments of food to the Jewish boys in the labor camps.

Our *Judenrat* has established contact with a Jewish go-between from Zloczow who is doing business with the German authorities at a labor camp in Latzk. Through the good offices of this go-between, the *Judenrat* of Sokal has come to an arrangement with the Germans. In return for a specified amount of cash, the Germans in the Latzk camp will exchange 40 young Jewish inmates for 40 other Jewish boys who are still "at large" in Sokal. This will enable the original group to go home and recuperate from the incredible hardships they have suffered at the camp. The *Judenrat* had collected the cash bribe from the parents of the boys who are now at the camp.

· · ·

The Jewish police, assisted by the Ukrainian policemen, have rounded up 40 boys who are to be transported to Latzk in place of the ones about to be released. The parents of the boys scheduled for release anxiously await the arrival of their sons. On April 26, the original 40 boys really arrive in Sokal. They fall into bed as soon as they get home. They are pale and emaciated, barely able to move. They can't even eat because their stomachs have shrunk from lack of nourishment.

[*It took these boys months to recover from their ordeal at Latzk. Their families were happy to have them back at home, but the parents of the new contingent that will go to replace them at the camp cried bitterly at the thought of what was in store for their own sons.*]

The parents of boys in two other labor camps have been summoned to *Judenrat* headquarters and asked to raise money so that their sons, too, can be released in exchange for others. The parents are glad to pay the required amount because they see that the arrangement really worked in the case of the Latzk camp. Many have sold their last possessions for money with which to buy food. Now, instead of using the money to get a little food for themselves, they give it to the *Judenrat* to rescue their sons from hell.

Many Jewish families no longer sleep at their own homes for fear that their children may be seized during the night and taken to a labor camp.

Sokal, May, 1942

The *Judenrat* is still collecting money from the parents of the boys in the labor camps, promising to get their sons released in exchange for other boys. But the catch is that the *Judenrat* cannot contact the go-between until the full amount of cash has been collected for the release of a specified contingent of boys. So the parents are pushing each other to make their payments to the *Judenrat* not today, but yesterday.

One warm, starlit night the Jewish police, working with a Ukrainian police detachment, fans out all over Sokal and drags 30 Jewish boys from their beds. It is understood that, in return for these boys, 30 others will be released from the labor camp in Koronice.

Early the next morning the chairman of the *Judenrat*, a lawyer by the name of Janowszinski, also takes with him the full amount of cash agreed upon for the release of 30 other boys. But this time the arrangement breaks down, The Germans at the camp accept the 30 new inmates and the money. However, they refuse to free the 30 "old" inmates who are supposed to be sent home in return for the money and for the new contingent of "Jew workers." In addition, the Germans detain Janowszinski and the two men from the Jewish police.

Two weeks later, thanks to the efforts of the Jewish go-between and the direct intervention of the German authorities in Sokal who do not want to lose the chairman of their *Judenrat*, Janowszinski, and the two men from the Jewish police, are released. But no boys at all are sent home from the Koronice camp. There are heartrending scenes at *Judenrat* headquarters. The parents who paid for the release of their sons want their money back. Some even accuse the *Judenrat* of having embezzled the money.

The food shipments to the camp inmates and the camp authorities have stopped. The *Judenrat* people are afraid to make the journey after what happened to Janowszinski and, even more so, after the tragic fate of Itsik Kiel. Kiel, a wealthy businessman who, among other things, owned a print shop, became director of the food supplies for the *Judenrat*. Instead of sending the sugar and bread rations allotted to the Jews of Sokal to the labor camps as bribes for the German and Ukrainian overseers, as had been the usual practice, Kiel decided to sell the rations on the black market. In this way, he reasoned, he could obtain substantial amounts of cash which in turn would buy larger quantities of more nourishing food that could be sent directly to the boys in the labor camps.

One day, Kiel sent a Jewish boy to deliver a bag of black market sugar to a Ukrainian. This was a fatal mistake on the part of Kiel; the Ukrainian happened to be in the pay of the Gestapo. The Ukrainian reported the boy; the boy was arrested and led the Gestapo to Kiel. Kiel was picked up at his print shop and placed under arrest. Both Kiel and the boy were shot. According to Shaye Krad, who works as a wagon driver for the local Gestapo, Kiel was savagely beaten and tortured for two weeks before he was executed.

• • •

The Gestapo headquarters here in Sokal houses the Gestapo prison for the entire district. When the prison is filled to capacity, the inmates are taken somewhere outside the town during the night and shot. That is how the Gestapo makes room for new prisoners.

• • •

The Jews in Sokal have lost an important source of nourishment. The Jewish community owned a total of 50 cows that produced milk and other dairy foods. Each month the *Judenrat* bribed the Ukrainian director of the regional farm administration to let the Jews keep the cows; the milk was needed especially for children and the sick. But on May 18th the *Judenrat* was ordered to have the cows delivered to the authorities in Patacise. The next morning, May 19th, I was delegated to carry out the order; it was assumed that, as a cattle dealer, I would know how to handle the animals. We are really upset but there is nothing we could have done to keep the cows.

Unlike Warsaw and several other Polish cities, Sokal has no ghetto. Jews are still permitted to live wherever they wish. But if a Gentile happens to take a fancy to the home of a Jew, he can go to the German housing authorities and put in a request for the apartment or the house. The Jew is then evicted and the Gentile can move in. Several Jews have set themselves up as negotiators for such cases. When a Jew is ordered out of his home because a Gentile wants to live there, these negotiators arrange for a suitable bribe and, as a rule, the Jew is permitted to remain.

I, too, narrowly escaped eviction. An official from the German housing authority appears at my house and orders me to move out with my family so that a Gentile can move in. I go straight to the director of the housing authority, a Pole named Winnikow, who worked as an engineer before the war. I ask him what this is all about. He, in turn, calls in one of his subordinates and asks him, "Who sent this man to me, and why?" The official explains that a certain Gentile woman wants my house because she has no place to live. But Winnikow is a decent man."Never mind," he says, and my family and I can stay on in our house— at least for the present.

What we all fear now in an *Aktion.* This is a Nazi term for a mass "operation" in which Jews of an entire locality are murdered on the spot or deported to an extermination camp such as Belzec (and a number of others) where they are shot or gassed if illness or starvation do not kill them first.

We are horror-stricken at the news about the deportations from other localities to the death camp of Belzec. Polish workers at the Sokal railroad station tell us that transports bound for Belzec are now passing through Sokal each day. The deportees are traveling under inhuman conditions—men, women and children crammed into airless cars in the unbearable heat, begging for a drink of water. It seems that these transports include Jews not only from Poland but from all over Nazi-occupied Europe: Holland, Belgium, France. It also appears that none of them even suspects the fate that is in store for them at their destination.

• • •

I have been receiving letters from my wife's parents and other relatives in Zolkiew. They are all starving. I send them food packages, two kilograms of wheat and other such delicacies. I address the packages to a Gentile from whom my in-laws can pick them up. Whenever my father-in-law receives a package from me, he considers himself a very lucky man. When I receive a letter from him informing me that one of my food packages has arrived, I am happy, too.

• • •

In the meantime, the German housing authorities have allowed a Gentile by the name of Bialoskurski to occupy most of my house, except for one single room, directly opposite the post office. This is the room in which I must live with my wife, Chana, our son, Chaim, who is now six, and our baby, Lifshe. Bialoskurski, who is a foreman at the forestry office, own several horses, which he keeps in my stable (where I used to have my cattle). The wagons from the forest ranger's office are brought into my courtyard each morning so the horses can be harnessed to them. Bialoskurski's wife has several Ukrainian students as boarders. Part of my backyard now belongs to her. I grow potatoes and beets in the part that has been left for my family and me.

• • •

My brother Shmelke is working at the Sokal railroad station together with 20 other young Jewish men. He helps unload coal arriving from points east. Shmelke is 27, still single and living with our parents and our two unmarried sisters, Yitte and Chaye Dvora. They all have moved in with our sister Leah and her in-laws, the Letzters, who live about three blocks from my house.

Shmelke stops at my house each morning on his way to work and again at seven each night on his way home. When he comes to see us in the morning, he has to unwind a mass of wires which the Bialoskurskis' Ukrainian boarders have wrapped around the latch of our door to lock us in for the night. The first time Shmelke found the door sealed from the outside, his heart almost stopped. He thought the Germans had picked us up. He certainly was relieved when he finally managed to undo the wires and found the four of us inside safe and sound.

• • •

I spend a good part of each day at the tavern of my neighbor Shlomo Schuman. There I get to hear the latest world news from the customers. Some of them have radios and can listen to the underground British news broadcasts. They know the latest devlopments on the battlefront. We are all anxiously waiting for the Allies to open a second front because only an Allied offensive from a second front will put a speedy end to this war and save us. Jews are also diligently reading the German newspapers and looking for hints between the lines about German setbacks. Even the children have become military and political experts. They know all about the fighting in Africa—Tobruk, Derna and El Alamein.

Our best-informed news reporters are Hirsch Teller, a tailor who has returned to Sokal from Lvov, and Efriam Windler, a watchmaker.

These two men have contacts with Poles from whom they hear the latest news.

• • •

Somehow, Jews in Sokal still manage to eat and keep a roof over their heads. They sell the last of their possessions for food and for cash with which they pay the *Judenrat* taxes. They sell clothing and furniture to Gentile stores and deal in foreign currency on the black market. Jewish women act as go-betweens for many business transactions between Gentiles and Jews. Mrs. Chamarinska, a Jewish woman who has converted to Christianity, sells me a liter of milk every other for my two children. We do this at the risk of our lives (and hers as well), for Jews caught buying milk, butter or eggs from a Gentile are liable to the death penalty under German law.

My mother and my sisters Yitte and Chaye Dvora have been working at odd jobs and have received three wagonloads of firewood as payment. The wood is now stored at Shmuel Letzter's house. My neighbor, Mr. Bialoskurski, offers to let the three women plant potatoes in a plot of ground on the forest ranger's estate if they will give him some of their firewood, which he badly needs.

• • •

My son Chaim has begun his Jewish studies. Yisroel, son of Yossele the teacher, comes to our room to instruct him. Yisroel looks like a character from a comic strip. He has shaved off his beard, but he sports two mustaches. He wears an ancient, crushed *yarmulka* and a *bekeshe*, a hasidic-type coat. His face is waxen and his belly bloated from malnutrition. My wife gives him a little food each time he comes so that he can maintain what little strength he has left. After he has finished eating, Yisroel recites the Grace after Meals with much feeling and thanks Chana profusely.

• • •

My father is sick in bed. I go to visit him every day at the Letzters. Jews are forbidden to use the sidewalks; they are permitted to walk only in the middle of the street. So I walk in the middle of the street, carrying a shovel, a pickaxe or a rake so that I should look as if I were on my way to a labor assignment. That is how all Jews act when they walk through the streets of Sokal.

At my father's house I meet his old friends from Krystynopol, his original home town: Yisroel Weinberg, Eliyahu Katz and Abramchele Katz. The old men complain about their troubles and reminisce about

the good old days when they were young. They sigh as they exchange
the latest reports of Jews being robbed or killed by Ukrainians. They
long for the day when we will have our revenge. In the course of the
conversation, my father says, "I already took my revenge on those
Ukrainians when I was a little boy. It seems that, back in Krystynopol, he was beaten up by a gang of Ukrainian rowdies and he
hit them back.

• • •

The Gestapo commander in Lvov, a man by the name of
Katzmann, pays regular inspection visits to Sokal. The day before he is
scheduled to arrive, the *Judenrat* spreads the word that Jews should
remain indoors the next day so it shouldn't occur to Katzmann that
there are too many Jews in Sokal.

The Gestapo has issued orders through the *Judenrat* that Jews are
forbidden to greet any German in the street, for how dare a Jewish
swine accost an Aryan superman? One day I pass a German in the
street and deliberately ignore him. So he gives me a slap in the face
and shouts, "Why don't you greet me, Jew-pig?" You can't win. . . .

• • •

The Jews have set up a post office of their own at *Judenrat* headquarters. Mail addressed to Jews living in Sokal arrives at the general
post office along with all the other mail, but the Gentile mailmen don't
feel like delivering mail to Jews. So the *Judenrat* sends someone to the
general post office to pick up mail addressed to Jews and takes it to the
Jewish post office. The mailman and postmaster of the Jewish post office is Hertz Pinias, a jack-of-all trades and black market operator
(specializing in foreign currency) from way back. In addition to
delivering mail to Jews, he sells them postcards and stamps which he
buys from the general post office.

Jews don't write many business letters nowadays. Jewish mail is
mostly an exchange of letters and postcards between relatives, informing each other in various prearranged codes that they have happily survived an *Aktion* in their town or that they know of a good place to hide
out if there is reason to fear an *Aktion*. If you stop receiving mail from
your relatives out of town, you know that they are probably no longer
among the living.

As I have already said, the room in which my family and I are now
living faces the general post office. So I don't need the *Judenrat*
postmaster to deliver my mail to me. The Polish mailman simply opens

the post office window facing my courtyard and hands me my letters. Most of them are from my in-laws in Zolkiew.

• • •

I see a Jewish boy among the Poles and Ukrainians who go to Wolyn each day for grain. I ask the boy where he lives. He tells me he is from Lvov. He lives on the same street as one of my mother's brothers, my uncle Nathan (Nutshe) Suchman. I ask the boy whether he knows him. He says he knows Nutshe and also Nutshe's children; they are all alive and well. The next week he brings me a letter from Nutshe, asking me to send him a little chaff. That's what is normally fed to cattle, but now it seems that Nutshe will be glad to have it as food for himself and his family. I tell the boy that next time he comes to Sokal, I will give him some chaff to take to my uncle in Lvov.

[*I have not seen the boy since. Perhaps he has been killed.*]

Sokal, June, 1942

The Jews of Sokal are working and starving. Jews by the hundreds are cleaning the streets and girls from some of the finest Jewish families are weeding the public lawns under the supervision of the Jewish police. The streets are burning with the summer heat. Poles and Ukrainians laugh and shout obscenities at the girls.

No one can sleep at night anymore. People are afraid there can be an *Aktion* at any time and they won't be able to escape.

• • •

A Jewish informer has reported to the Gestapo that the silver of the Hasidic rebbe of Belz, who has fled from Sokal, has been gathered up by his followers on Sokal and buried somewhere. Yaakov Yoshe, the sexton, and Leizer Melammed, the cantor were picked up by the Gestapo, along with our little *dayyan*,* and ordered to take the Gestapo to the place where the rebbe's silver had been hidden. The silver was buried in the ground beneath the floor of the synagogue near the wooden bridge that spans the River Bug. The Gestapo men dug out the silver objects with their bare hands. Then they shot Yaakov Yoshe, Leizer Melammed and the little *dayyan*.

• • •

---

* A rabbinical judge who helps decide questions of religious law.

The Jews anxiously await reports from the world outside. Some of our people are optimists; they urge us to keep our courage because Hitler can't possibly last much longer. Others are pessimists; they tell us that life isn't worth living anymore.

There are reports in the German newspapers that make your blood run cold. The newspapers proudly proclaim that the city of Lublin has become *judenrein*, literally, "free of Jews," as if the Jews were so many parasites to be eliminated. This means that there are no more Jews left in that ancient community, whose great Talmudical academy produced so many world-famous rabbis and Talmudic scholars. The papers report that 54,000 Jews from Lublin have been "resettled" in a place called Maidanek.*

* * *

Hans Frank, the governor of the German section of Poland, has made an inspection tour of eastern Galicia. He reports that the only Jews left in the region are the "good" Jews, that is the Jews who are doing slave labor at railroad stations and in other jobs essential to the Nazi war effort.

* * *

I'm having trouble with my Gentile neighbors. One of them, Mrs. Stechnik, a hunchbacked hag, accuses me of having stolen her firewood and stored it in the basement of my house (which has been virtually taken over by the Bialoskurskis). I swear to her that the only firewood I have in my place is my own. I take her to my storage space in the basement to prove it. To my amazement, the storage space is empty. Not a splinter of my firewood is left. Someone must have stolen it.

Mrs. Stechnik then says she will do me a favor; she will not report *me* to the Gestapo for having stolen *her* firewood. She has it all wrong: I think that she and her son Janek are the thieves. *They* have stolen *my* firewood. I figured I had enough firewood stored up to last me a month. Now I don't have any left. But I am afraid to start an argument with Mrs. Stechnik.

I have met two Ukrainian girls from Zolkiew who are attending high school here in Sokal. I make an arrangement with them that they

---

* Maidanek was a death camp where 125,000 Jews perished. Only a few hundred inmates were still alive when the camp was liberated by Russian troops on July 24, 1944.

should take a package of flour to my in-laws in Zolkiew every Saturday when they go home for the weekend. I promise to pay them 20 zlotys for each package they deliver. The very first Saturday, while the girls are in my room waiting for me to pack up the flour, who comes in but Mrs. Stechnik! She starts yelling at the two girls that they shouldn't do business with Jews. The girls run away and never return to pick up the package for my in-laws.

• • •

A Gentile woman wants to sell me vegetables from her pushcart, but another Gentile woman screams at her, "How dare you sell your vegetables to a Jew?"

• • •

A transport of 500 Jews that arrived in the town of Belz has now been shipped to the death camp of Belzec. The transport had been supposed to go to Belzec in the first place but had been sent to Belz due to some breakdown in German efficiency. Now the 500 have been taken to Belzec, where they were moved directly to the gas chambers.

• • •

Rishe, the baker's widow, is gone. She owned the one bakery still left in town where Jews could buy bread. She had been allowed to continue her business because she paid protection money to the Ukrainians. But the other day the Gestapo broke into her store and arrested her along with her two daughters. We hear that Rishe's house has been confiscated and that she and her daughters have been shot.

Sokal, July, 1942

The German army confiscated approximately 1,000 head of cattle from farms in the Urubieszow district and brought the animals to the Sokal railroad station for shipment to Germany. The Germans kept the cattle fenced in near the railroad platform waiting for a train to become available. Every day the *Judenrat* had to send 30 Jews to the station to feed and tend the cattle. Every day these Jews returned home beaten black and blue by the German overseers. So the more affluent Jews decided they would be better off if they paid other Jews to go to the station and care for the cattle in their place. I must say they paid their substitutes handsomely for the trouble and the beatings.

One afternoon as I was standing outside my house, Long Meir, Reb Yehuda's son, ran up to me, his face ashen with terror. He had just come back from the station where he had been helping tend the cattle.

Now the cattle were finally being loaded aboard a train for shipment to Germany. But it seemed that not only cattle were being herded into the train. Zulchinsky, the Gentile cattle dealer and wholesale butcher, signaled to Meir to run away as fast as he could because Jews were being loaded into the boxcars along with the cattle. That is all Meir could tell me, but I could imagine the rest. Among those deported on that cattle train was a son of a the *shohet* (ritual slaughterer) Dobrodon, one of the best-known Talmudic experts in Sokal.

• • •

The *Judenrat* has issued an order that every Jew must have a number sewn on his or her Star of David armband. This number must be registered also in the person's documents along with the letter "A" for *Arbeiter* (worker). Anyone without such a number will be sent directly to a labor camp.

The Jews have been rushing to the labor office of the *Judenrat* to get their numbers. Some are willing to pay for receiving a number as quickly as possible.

I, too, report to the *Judenrat* labor office for a number. The director of the *Judenrat* labor office is a lawyer by the name of Steiner; he is not originally from Sokal. He is an assimilationist and was not particularly interested in Jewish affairs before the war. But he has taken the job with the *Judenrat* because he thinks it will save him and his family from deportation.

He asks me where I am employed at present. I tell him that I have been working for Zulchinsky, the cattle dealer and wholesale butcher. (Zulchinsky has been signing as my employer on my *Meldekarte*.) When Steiner asks me exactly what kind of work I do for Zulchinsky, I think fast and say that I'm a gardener on Zulchinsky's farm outside town. Steiner replies that gardening isn't really considered work under the new regulations. "I'll be put to work on the highways," he says. But I don't like the idea of being assigned to highway construction because I could be shot by any German or Ukrainian who happens to pass along the highway and is seized by a sudden desire to pick off a Jew. I ask Steiner to give me a number even though he doesn't consider gardening a job, but to no avail.

Finally, I decide to go directly to Zulchinsky for help. My family has known him for a long time; we did business with him before the war.

When I arrive at Zulchinsky's farm, I find a couple of dozen Jews already busy working there. I ask to see Zulchinsky and he comes, looking healthy and well-fed while I am skin and bones, hungry and in rags with the mark of shame on my armband.

"What can I do for you, Moshe?" he asks. To my surprise, he is talking to me in Yiddish. I ask him to write a note to Dr. Steiner at the *Judenrat* labor office, telling him to stop harassing me and to give me what I want without further delay. Zulchinsky takes a sheet of paper, scribbles a few lines on it, slips it into an envelope and hands the envelope to me.

I bid Zulchinsky a quick and grateful good-bye and rush back to Steiner's office. When Steiner sees the signature of Zulchinsky, whom he knows as a wealthy, influential Gentile, he begins to look uneasy and asks me again exactly what I want from him. I tell him that all I want is a registration number. Steiner calls in one of his office assistants, a man named Singer, and, within minutes, I have my number and can go home.

• • •

I'm having trouble with my neighbor Mrs. Stechnik again. For the past few weeks I've been checking my little vegetable patch in the backyard to see whether my potatoes and beets are ready for picking. One morning I discover that someone has dug up most of my potatoes. Hese Letzter, my sister Leah's sister-in-law, tells me that, on her way to work, she saw Mrs. Stechnik digging in my vegetable patch. But again, I can't afford a fight with Mrs. Stechnik, so I have to keep quiet while she comes out each morning when she thinks I'm not looking and digs up some more of my potatoes.

• • •

Hungry Jews are going from house to house begging for potato peelings. Since we no longer have any potatoes, Chana and I are giving these poor people beets from our garden. They thank us profusely. On Sabbath afternoons, when I sit with my neighbor Shlomo Schuman in front of his house, it breaks my heart to watch him cut two loaves of bread into tiny pieces which he hands to the hungry, emaciated Jewish children that pass by. Shlomo is the only Jewish man I know in town who thinks of such little acts of natural kindness.

Prices are rising all the time. The Jews have to pay three times as much as Gentiles for food.

• • •

An *Aktion* has been going on in Lvov for two solid weeks. Gentiles who have come here from Lvov shake their heads in disbelief and horror as they give us the reports.

Sokal, August, 1942

The Jews gobble up every scrap of news they can get from newspapers or from people who seem to be in the know. We are all waiting for the Allies to open a second front somewhere. The are reports that the British have attempted a landing in France, on the Channel coast, but that they failed to establish a foothold there. The Germans claim they have killed huge numbers of Allied troops and captured many Canadians.* The Germans are delighted because they think this proves how good their *Festung Europa* (Fortress Europe) really is. They boast that the German fortifications on the Channel coast will keep the Allies from opening a second front there.

We Jews do not believe the German newspapers. We think that this Allied landing was intended merely as a kind of rehearsal, part of an Allied war of nerves against the Germans, forcing the Germans to maintain a large army all along the Channel coast of France. The Jews in Sokal are happy because all this indicates that the Allies are at least doing something.

We are also keeping up with the news from the Russian front. The reports from there are satisfactory. The Russians are keeping the German forces at bay. The Jews are confident that the Russian terrain and climate will eventually force the Nazi murderers to retreat. Only . . . sometimes I wonder whether we Jews will live to see it.

• • •

At two o'clock one morning we have an air raid. Russian planes are circling overhead. The people pour from their houses, thinking they will be safer outdoors when the bombs begin to fall and the buildings collapse. But nothing happens; it is probably just a reconnaissance flight.

• • •

It is now 14 months since the Russians abandoned Sokal to the Germans. According to the German newspapers, the Russians have no more weapons left with which to fight. But we know better, now that we have seen those Russian bombers that are obviously capable of

---

* This was an abortive Allied "commando" landing at Dieppe under Lord Louis Mountbatten.

flying distances of 2,000 kilometers; that's how far the Russian battle lines are from Sokal.

The Ukrainians seem depressed; they see that the Russians are still able to give as they get. The Ukrainians are behaving better towards us Jews than in the past. Still, we can't work up too much optimism. We fear we may not live to see our deliverance even though we want so badly to be alive when this war finally ends.

• • •

All kinds of rumors are making the rounds, some of them probably started by well-meaning people, including Gentiles, who would like to make us feel better. One such report comes from a German labor foreman by the name of Pollack, who seems to be sorry for the Jews. He says he has learned from a reliable source that Hitler has decided to stop killing Jews. Pollack first told this story at the tavern of my friend Issachar Spalter, where he is a regular customer. I have heard similar reports from Shlomo Schuman. The mood at Schuman's tavern is always cheerful. A Gentile by the name of Shulkevitch, who has taken over the soda water bottling plant formerly owned by Schuman's son-in-law, frequently stops at Schuman's tavern with Pollack for a round of drinks. At one of these sessions, Pollack says that the death camp at Belzec and its gas chambers have been shut down because the Germans aren't killing Jews anymore.

Efraim Windler, the watchmaker, reports a piece of news he claims to have gotten from a Gestapo men: the Jews of Sokal will be allowed to survive because the Germans consider them to be "good Jews," assets to the German war effort. Maybe our deliverance is really closer than we think. The very thought helps us forget about our hunger, at least for a short time.

But my brother Shmelke comes home from his work at the railroad station with a very different story. Polish railroad workers have told him that even larger transports of Jews are being sent to Belzec than before.

Also, we hear that Jews are still being killed in the streets of Lvov.

• • •

Something terrible happened on August 15th, the Sabbath before the beginning of Elul, the month of preparations for the solemn High Holiday season. A small-town Hasidic *rebbe* had been conducting services every Sabbath for a prayer group at what was once the home of Sokal's principal rabbi.

I was not at the services, but at my friend Shlomo Schuman's house. I do not dare go to any synagogue services nowadays because the Nazis could raid the synagogue and arrest the worshippers. A man bursts into Schuman's living room. "The Germans got the *rebbe's* prayer group!" he shouted.

Shlomo and I were sure the raid on the prayer group signaled the start of an *Aktion*. This hadn't happened, but what did happen was bad enough. The Gestapo arrested the 31 men and boys at the service, along with the *rebbe*, pushed them into trucks and drove them to Gestapo headquarters. There they were ordered to strip down to their underwear. After that, they were herded back into the trucks, taken to a place outside town and shot. A Ukrainian policeman who witnessed the scene reported that the *rebbe's* youngest son cursed the Gestapo before he died. "Your end is near!" the boy shouted. "And all German people will have to pay for the innocent blood you have shed!" In reply, a Gestapo man split the boy's head with an axe instead of waiting to shoot him along with the others.

The next day, Sunday, August 16th, a Pole was seen going around Sokal selling eyeglasses. The glasses had been taken from the Jews of the *rebbe's* prayer group.

• • •

On Friday afternoon a rumor races through town that an *Aktion* is imminent. Everyone is looking for a place to hide. Six Jews and six Gentiles have been arrested; that same evening they were taken to places outside town by Ukrainian militiamen and shot. The Ukrainians apparently want to eliminate beggars, so they lump Gentile beggars with Jews who look just as ragged and starved, and they shoot them together.

• • •

One Sunday my brother Shmelke stops at my house as usual on his way home from the railroad station. He seems ready to burst into tears. "Shmelke! What happened?" I ask him. It takes quite a while before Shmelke is able to talk. He pulls a bundle of papers from his bag and hands it to me. He says these are documents found in a railroad car he and other Jewish workers had to clean today. The car was part of a train that returned empty from the death camp of Belzec. Shmelke and his friends also found American dollar bills and Soviet ruble notes, torn into small pieces. Apparently the deportees who owned these foreign bills destroyed them on the journey to Belzec so that the Nazi and Ukrainian murderers should not be able to use them. In addition, Shmelke and his friends picked up children's clothes and identification papers issued in the city of Kovel, bearing an official Nazi seal and giving the age of the holders as 18. "Look at these papers," says Shmelke. "Do you still think it's worthwhile to go on living?"

• • •

The Gestapo has notified the *Judenrat* that all Jews engaged in work essential to the German war effort must have special Gestapo seals placed on their identification papers. These official seals exempt them from deportation if there is an *Aktion.* What actually happens is that the first to receive these seals are the board members and workers of the *Judenrat.* Jews working at the brick factory, at the railroad station and at the *Judenrat's* Jewish post office come next in the order of priority. After them come those ordinary Jews who have paid the *Judenrat* to see that they get these seals which they hope will save their lives.

A brisk business in Gestapo seals is developing. My supposed employment on Zulchinsky's farm does not entitle me to classification as an "essential" worker. But the word comes that two additional workers are needed at the railroad station. Joshua Markel, who is working at the station, tells my neighbor Haskel Pollak that he could get one man placed on the railroad workers' list in return for a payment of 350 zlotys. However, Joshua says he is willing to make an exception in our case and put both Pollak and me on the workers' list without asking either one of us for money.

Early the next morning Pollak and I report for work on the railroad. The stationmaster takes one look at us and says, "I need strong men, not weaklings like you." So we go home in disgrace and I don't get my Gestapo seal that day.

[I later learn that being rejected by the stationmaster saved my life. Had I been working at the job for which I reported, I would have been put on one of the trains bound for Belzec.]

Sokal, end of August, 1942.

Something is about to happen. The *Judenrat* has sent out girls to take a census of Sokal's Jewish community: how many persons in each family, how many children and how many old people. I think the Germans have ordered the *Judenrat* to take these statistics so they can make more efficient plans for an *Aktion.*

The Gentiles seem to have agreed among themselves not to buy anything more from Jews because Jews will soon be gone and then they will be able to take anything the Jews will leave behind without having to pay a penny.

The other day a Gentile woman looked at my baby daughter Lifshe, shook her head and said, "Little girl, why were you ever born?" A Gentile came into my room and said, "Give me some of your furniture. You won't need it where you're going."

• • •

The Jews are looking for places to hide when the *Aktion* comes. Some are digging bunkers. A friend of mine suggests that he and I ger permits to travel from village to village as rag peddlers. In this way the two of us could leave Sokal and go underground in some village as soon as we hear that an *Aktion* is imminent. But when what happens to my family? Perhaps, if there is an *Aktion*, I should lock Chana and the two children inside our room while I stay outside. The Germans may be satisfied to get me and not look any further. Then at least my wife and children will have a chance to survive and tell our story to the world when the war is over. But I dismiss this plan out of hand because our neighbor Mrs. Stechnik would turn in Chana and the children in to the Gestapo who may be satisfied to get me and not look any further. Then at least my wife and children will have a chance to survive and tell our story to the world when the war is over.

• • •

I go see another Gentile neighbor, Mrs. Horodejcyk, who owns the building in which the general post office is located. I ask her whether my family and I could hide in the stable behind her house if there is an *Aktion*. She says it would be all right with her. But a few days later Shlomo Schuman tells me that he overheard Mrs. Horodejcyk's daughter say to her mother, "So, Maltz expects me to risk my neck so he can save himself and his family? Well, you can count me out!" So much for Mrs. Horodejcyk.

• • •

Jews are taking their belongings to the homes of Gentile acquaintances for safekeeping so that, if there is an *Aktion*, they can go to their hiding places as quickly as possible.

Sokal, September, 1942

The *Judenrat* is collecting more taxes to bribe the Germans.

Everybody has been asked to pay as much as he can possibly spare; if we pay the Germans off, we are told, there won't be an *Aktion* here in Sokal.

I owe the *Judenrat* 50 zlotys in back taxes but don't have the cash. My family and I have been living from the sale of our old clothes and other belongings, but now the Germans are no longer willing to buy anything from us. They expect to get our possessions free of charge when we are gone.

At any rate, a member of the Jewish police comes to my room with a summons from the tax office of the *Judenrat*. I report to Pessel, the pharmacist, who is now the *Judenrat*'s director of revenue. Pessel asks me why I haven't paid my tax. I promise to raise the cash within a few days, but he immediately sends me to the detention room at *Judenrat* headquarters.

I found another Jew there, serving time for the same offense—failure to pay his tax. He says he came to Sokal a short time ago, and he curses the *Judenrat*. But his own brother is working there, and as a result he is released in short order, leaving me locked up alone in the detention room.

I worry what will happen if there is an *Aktion* this evening, while I'm still locked up. Since I am in the *Judenrat* building, the Germans will probably get me at once, and how will my wife find a hiding place for herself and the children if I'm not there? I break into a cold sweat. Then I pull myself together. I slip a note through a crack under the door of the detention room. The note is addressed to Janowszinski, the chairman of the *Judenrat*, asking him to contact a friend of mine who will pay the tax for me. Meanwhile, Janowszinski can have my watch as security if he releases me at once.

When Janowszinski learns that I have been locked up for a measly 50 zlotys, he immediately orders my release. He does not accept my watch.

• • •

There are rumors that Russian partisan fighters have been seen in the woods outside Sokal. Abraham, the son of Baruch with the goatee, who had been hiding out in the woods, reported to *Judenrat* headquarters that a civilian carrying a gun stopped him and questioned him in Russian, asking him, among other things, how many Germans there were in Sokal. Abraham was a fool. He thought that if he reported this incident also to the Gestapo, he would receive a reward for reporting the presence of an enemy spy. The Germans listened to his story, but instead of giving him a reward, they placed him under arrest and shot him a few days later.

. . .

Two teenage boys from the town of Pritzk have come to Sokal. They report that the Germans and the Ukrainians have rounded up all the Jews of Pritzk, Yuvanich, Ludmir and other localities in the area. But these boys managed to escape.

. . .

The Jews in Sokal are busier than ever making arrangements for places to hide when (and I no longer say "if") there is an *Aktion*. My plan is that our family should not hide together in one place but should be scattered, so that our whole family will not be wiped out at one blow. At least some of us must remain as living witnesses to the tragedy that befell our people.

My brother Shmelke has prepared the cellar of the home of Ivanich, a Gentile acquaintance, on New Street, as a shelter for our sisters, Leah and Yitte, and Leah's little daughter Feyge Chashe. Chana and our two children, our sister Dvora and I will go the home of Mrs. Francisca Halamajowa on No. 4 Street of Our Lady.

Francisca Halamajowa, 1946.

We have known Mrs. Halama-jowa for some years. She is a Polish Catholic woman in her late fifties who lived in Germany for a time and learned to speak a perfect German. She was married to a Ukrainian whom she threw out of her house because he was a Nazi, which she definitely is not.

This is how we came to the arrangement with Mrs. Halamajowa: Some time ago, my mother went to sound out Mrs. Halamajowa about a place where we could hide during an *Aktion*. Mrs. Halamajowa took Mother to her pigsty next to her home and pointed to a hayloft that could be reached by climbing a ladder from the pigsty below. "That's where my daughter Hela hid out when the Germans were picking up Ukrainians for slave labor," she explained. "You and your husband could stay there, too, Mrs. Maltz." Mother was surprised and deeply touched by Mrs. Halamajowa's offer. "You'd really give us shelter at your own home, in your own hayloft?" she asked. "Why not? Mrs. Halamajowa replied.

On her way home, my mother stopped at my house to tell me about her visit to Mrs. Halamajowa. I gave my mother a ring, and enough material for a blouse, and said to her, "Please take these things to Mrs. Halamajowa as gifts from your family and tell her that if there is an *Aktion*, your youngest daughter and son Moshe with his family will be coming to the hayloft along with you."

My sister Leah accompanied Mother to Mrs. Halamajowa's house. Mrs. Halamajowa would not take our gifts, but Mother left the ring and the material with her anyway. Mrs. Halamajowa took Mother and Leah outside and showed them a path around the back of her house that led directly to the pigsty. "Better use this roundabout way when you move into my pigsty, Mrs. Maltz," she said. "People are less likely to see you then."

The next day Leah took me to Mrs. Halamajowa's house by this arranged roundabout route so I should know the way also. The house virtually touches the east bank of the River Bug that formerly marked the border between the Russian and German sectors of Poland.

On the way to Mrs. Halamajowa's house we saw a number of Jews hurrying past us along the streets near the river. They were probably looking for hiding places. Some were carrying packages; perhaps they were taking their belongings to the homes of Gentile friends for safekeeping.

• • •

The Jews are selling the last of their belongings for a few zlotys. My parents have sold their sewing machine. Riftche, Yisroel Weinberg's wife, brought two Gentile women from Wloclawek to my parents' room at the Letzters' place to look at the machine. The women started to bargain with my mother. Mother asked for 2,000 zlotys, but the women wanted to pay only 1,800. It looked as if there would be no deal.

Then two Ukrainian policemen came in, acting as if they were slightly tipsy. "You have a sewing machine for sale?" one of them asked my mother. They looked over the machine and offered Mother

1,000 zlotys. Mother understood at once that these policemen had been sent to her by the Gentile women. Under the circumstances, she had no other choice but to take the 1,000 zlotys. The Ukrainians picked up two Jews from the street to take the machine away. Mother could see the two women from Wloclawek waiting across the street with a horse-drawn cart. The Jews loaded the machine onto the cart and off the two women went with their lucky purchase.

• • •

On Saturday I go to pay a Sabbath visit to my parents. As I approach the Letzters' place, our friend Gershfeld comes running toward me. "Get away from here!" he says, unable to catch his breath. "A Ukrainian policeman is picking up Jews for work!"

I turn on my heel and walk off in another direction, toward the house of my friend Leibush Reisler. Suddenly I hear a voice behind me shouting, "Halt!" I turn around. It is a Ukrainian policeman with a bicycle. He prods me with the butt of his rifle. "Who are you running away from, Jew-boy?" he wants to know. I answer that I'm not running away from anyone; I am just taking a walk. He grabs me and shoves me into the Letzters' house. Mottel Gelbart, who is married to Letzter's daughter Hesse, is also there. Another Ukrainian policeman enters the house with two other Jews.

The Ukrainians push Mottel and me out of the house. Mottel and I are really frightened now. If the Ukrainians just want some Jews for labor, they can go to the *Judenrat* headquarters and the Jewish police will get them the manpower. If Ukrainian policemen go around picking up Jews in the street, it may be the beginning of an *Aktion*. I see several German policemen coming toward us. Now I am sure that Mottel and I are about to be led to our death. But then I see Mottel's wife, Hesse, talking with Bronstein, the chief of the Jewish police. This makes me feel a little better. Shmuel Letzter walks up to one of the Germans and says a few words to him. Then Bronstein turns around and walks away.

The Ukrainians order Mottel and me to look straight ahead and keep going. We end up at the *targevicze*, the open market square where cattle are sold. A peasant wagon is waiting there, also two pigs, one cow and one sheep. The Ukrainians give us our orders: we are to take the animals to the German police. One Ukrainian asks Mottel and me whether we have any experience in cattleherding. Mottel says, "Yes." And so Mottel Gelbart and I walk through the streets of Sokal on a

Sabbath day, marching two pigs, one cow and one sheep to the slaughter.

At police headquarters the German policemen take the animals from us but they are not through with us yet. One of the Germans asks which of us can take the cow to a farm in the village of Potacic, about three kilometers away. I say I'll take the cow. I am ready to do anything to get away from these Germans. But I want to make sure that Mottel also gets away, so I tell the Germans I need another experienced cowherd to help me with the cow.

Mottel and I take the cow to her destination, and then we're told we are free to go home.

• • •

A bunker has been built under the ground floor of Shmuel Letzter's house. The entrance to this bunker is through my parents' room and is covered by several boards. Since my father is sick, Mother has decided against going to Mrs. Halamajowa's hayloft if there is an *Aktion*. It would be much too crowded, and too little air, for my father. The same would be true of the Letzters' bunker. So Mother has prepared a hiding place for Father and herself in the Letzters' attic instead.

• • •

The Jews are getting ready for the worst. The members and staff of the *Judenrat* have prepared signs to place on the doors of their homes stating that they are working for the *Judenrat*. They think that this will make them privileged characters in the eyes of the Germans and save them from deportation when the *Aktion* comes.

You can almost touch the atmosphere of doom hanging over Sokal. Posters have appeared in the streets proclaiming that if there is a *Judenaussiedlung*—an evacuation of Jews, which is a nicer word for "deportation," Gentiles will be forbidden to give shelter to Jews, to accept Jewish property for safekeeping or to buy articles offered for sale by the departing Jews.

Now everybody knows what is ahead; we don't have to ask the *Judenrat* anymore.

Some people still try to persuade themselves that it's all a false alarm. Look, they argue, the German Provincial Commissioner has just ordered a new suit from a Jewish tailor in town, and one of the "blacks" (that's what we call the Ukrainian police because of their uniforms) has ordered a pair of custom-made boots from a Jewish shoemaker. Would they be doing that sort of business with Jews if they were planning an *Aktion*?

. . .

On Monday, September 14, the day after Rosh HaShanah, my brother Shmelke comes from the railroad station with ominous news. The stationmaster, a Pole, has told him in strict confidence, that railroad cars are already being sent to Sokal for the Jews. These are special cars used by the Germans to transport Jews to the death camps.

The Germans need all their rolling stock for the war effort. The railroad station and the newspapers are full of announcements that "the wheels are rolling for victory" and that trains should be used only for "essential" travel. And yet the Germans are setting aside special trains to deport Jews.

. . .

All this has been happening during the Jewish season of solemn introspection and penitence, the period between Rosh HaShanah, the Jewish New Year, and Yom Kippur, the Day of Atonement. Members of the *Judenrat* keep asking my brother Shmelke whether the rumors about the special trains are based on fact. From what the *Judenrat* people seem to know (or perhaps from what they want us to know), the *Aktion* is still some time away.

Nevertheless, on the night of Tuesday, September 15, I lock up our room and, together with my wife Chana, our two children and my sister Chaye Dvora, I set out for our hiding place in the hayloft of Mrs. Halamajowa's pigsty. We three grown-ups and Chaim (with Chana carrying Lifshe in her arms), walk single file, about 100 meters apart, so that we shouldn't attract attention.

Mrs. Halamajowa takes us to her pigsty and we climb up the ladder to the hayloft. The five of us lie down in the hay in pitch darkness. Not until the next morning, when the cracks in the wooden walls admit a little daylight, are we able to examine our shelter more closely.

Later that morning, Mrs. Halamajowa climbs up the ladder to the hayloft with some food for us.

Chana, the children, Chaye Dvora and I lie in the hay all day long, waiting for the storm to begin, but nothing happens.

In the hayloft, Thursday, September 17, 1942

At five o'clock this morning we hear gunfire from the streets and from the direction of the fields behind us. Mrs. Halamajowa brings us our breakfast and informs us that the *Aktion* has begun. The Germans, accompanied by members of the Jewish police, are all over town, picking up Jews. We don't touch Mrs. Halamajowa's food; we have lost our appetites.

At nine o'clock we hear a guttural German voice from Mrs. Halamajowa's courtyard. "Any Jews in there?" Mrs. Halamajowa calmly replies, in German, "No, sir."

At eleven o'clock Mrs. Halamajowa is back with the latest news. She says that her neighbor, who shares her house with her, has found out that we have gone into hiding in some part of her home. So he sent his twelve-year-old son with a message to Mrs. Halamajowa, strongly urging her to throw the Jews out. The neighbor turns out to be none other than the stationmaster at the railroad station where my brother Shmelke is working. How could the stationmaster possibly have found out where we have gone?

[*Much later, Shmelke confessed that he was to blame. In an unguarded moment, he had said to the stationmaster that if there would be an* Aktion, *he, Shmelke, would not have to worry about his brother and sister because they had found a good hiding place. Shmelke even told the stationmaster the name of our benefactor. He had thought that the stationmaster, a quiet elderly man, felt sorry for the Jews and would be happy if we survived the war. Unfortunately, Shmelke had too high an opinion of this stationmaster. It seems that the stationmaster knew we had arrived at our hiding place when he heard Lifshe crying, and he was afraid that if the Germans caught us and Mrs. Halamajowa, he, too, might get into trouble as an "accomplice" of a Polish woman who gave shelter to Jews.*]

Mrs. Halamajowa is distraught. She says we should leave her hayloft and hide among the tall ears of corn near her backyard until the *Aktion* is over and we can go home again.

I plead with her to let us stay in her hayloft. If she puts us out, we're lost because the Germans will be searching for Jews in every corner of her place, not excluding her backyard.

She leaves us. But in a little while she is back. "I've decided to let you stay," she says. "But my daughter Hela is the secretary at the post office. I don't want her to get into trouble if the Germans find you here. So I have my bags packed; if the Germans find you, I'll take all the blame for sheltering you and I'll tell the Germans to take me wherever they'll be taking you." What a courageous woman!

Mrs. Halamajowa gives us virtually hour-by-hour reports on what is happening outside. At one o'clock in the afternoon she comes up to tell us that the *Aktion* appears to be over. The German plan for this particular type of *Aktion* was to pick up 2,000 Jews, and it seems that the Germans achieved this "quota." At four o'clock she informs us that Jews—including children, old people and invalids—are being marched to the railroad station in one long column, extending, she says, over at least two kilometers. She even tells us the names of some friends of ours whom she spotted in that death march.

In the evening, Mrs. Halamajowa's daughter Hela visits us in the hayloft. She says that, looking out from her office window which faces the courtyard of my house, she saw a German, accompanied by Hersh Klar, a member of the Jewish police, attempting to break into my room. Klar yanked at the latch of the entrance, so now it is no longer locked. Hela also reports having seen members of the *Judenrat* staff and of the Jewish police escorting the Germans through the streets of the city and actively helping them round up Jews.

That night we are unable to sleep.

In the hayloft and at home, Friday, September 18, 1942

We have an unexpected early morning visitor at the hayloft; my brother Shmelke. Mrs. Halamajowa gave him special permission to come to us on his way to work. What a relief to see him alive and well! He tells us that he and 16 other Jews survived the *Aktion* at the station, hidden inside the huge water tank that feeds the water into the steam locomotives. (The water tank happened to be empty.) He, Shmelke, gave one of the Polish railroad workers, a man by the name of Kovalcziz, 1,000 zlotys so that he, Shmelke, and his friends could stay in the tank until the *Aktion* was over and it would be safe for them to come out.

From this hiding place, Shmelke and the others saw how Jews, men, women, children, the old and the sick, all of them together, were packed into railroad cars. The *Judenrat* people stood on the platform, tossing loaves of bread into the cars so that the passengers should have something to eat during their long journey. Then the cars were sealed and the windows barred with barbed wire to make sure no one escaped from the death train.

Shmelke does not know whether our parents, Leah and Yitte have survived. He is utterly broken. He says he could hear the moans and

Shmelke (indicated by arrow) with members of the Mizrachi group in Sokal before the outbreak of World War II.

cries of the Jews from his own safe shelter in the water tank. He saw a girl, shot by the Germans, lying on the station platform in a pool of blood. He was close enough to see a document beside the body; it said that the girl was from Tartakov.

But now, at least for the time being, the *Aktion* is over and we can go home. At eight o'clock, after Shmelke has left, we go down from the hayloft to the pigsty and from there to Mrs. Halamajowa's house. She serves us breakfast, gives Lifshe a bath and is in a most cheerful mood.

We bid farewell to Mrs. Halamajowa. She follows us, making sure that we shouldn't be too conspicuous. The streets are deserted, except for some Gestapo men who stare at us and laugh. They're probably thinking, "So you Jews got away this time. But rest assured that we won't let you off so easily next time around. You'll be on the next transport."

We pass a wagon piled high with bodies and guarded by members of the Jewish police. [*Later, I hear that 140 Jews were killed in the city during the* Aktion.]

We arrive at our room. The door, as Hela Halamajowa has already told us, is unlocked. The place is a shambles. We try to create a little order. We close the windows, sweep the floor.

On my way to the Letzters' house to see how my parents are, I stop at *Judenrat* headquarters for more news. I hear that the *Judenrat* people who posted the *Judenrat* signs on the doors of their homes were not harmed.

From other bits of information, I can piece the picture together. All the "good" Jewish workers with the Gestapo seals showing that they were "essential" to the German war effort, went to their places of work as usual on the morning of the *Aktion*. Some of them had spent the previous night at the brick factory where they worked by day, bringing their families with them so that they, too, would be safe. But the Gestapo, perversely, went first to the places, such as the brick factory, where the "good" Jews with the Gestapo seals were working. And so all "good" Jews, including those working at the Jewish post office, were deported. Of the "privileged characters," only the members and employees of the *Judenrat* and their immediate families have survived.

When the Jews caught in the *Aktion* were led to the railroad station, anyone who didn't move fast enough to suit the Germans were gunned down on the spot. One woman couldn't walk very fast because she had her baby nursing at her breast. So the Germans shot her, but the baby remained at its dead mother's breast and continued to suckle.

Before they were taken to the railroad station, all the Jews who had been rounded up in the *Aktion* were assembled in the marketplace near the town hall and ordered to squat on their knees. Efraim Windler, the watchmaker, had made a masterpiece of a gold ring for Seemann, the most notorious of the Gestapo gangsters, as a bribe, in return for Seemann's promise that if there was an *Aktion*, he, Windler, and his family, would be spared. As a result, Windler did not think it necessary to go into hiding with his family. But the Gestapo took the Windlers to the marketplace along with all the other Jews. Windler caught sight of Seemann and ran over to him. "Remember the promise you made to me?" he asked the Gestapo officer. Seemann's answer was to raise his gun and put a bullet through Windler's head right there in the marketplace.

Other Jews gave all their belongings to Gentiles in return for a promise of shelter. The Germans accepted the gifts, took in the Jews but then handed them over to the Gestapo.

Finally I arrived at Letzter's place. Everyone—the Letzter family,

Lea, Fay (Fayge Chashe), daughter Debra, 1992.

my parents, Leah, Yitte, Chaye Dvora and little Feyge Chashe—is alive and well. But many of my parents' neighbors are gone. Mottel Gelbart tells how on Thursday morning, before he could move into his bunker, the Gestapo broke into his house and took him away with dozens of other Jews. Mottel was taken to the railroad station, where he was saved from deportation at the last minute by a miracle.

It seems that the *Judenrat* people, in a last-ditch effort to save at least some of the Jews who were about to be deported, put in a telephone call to *Oberleutnant* (First Lieutenant) Krupa, an Austrian officer who was the commandant of a labor camp in Zavonia, near Most. Krupa was known as a good man who helped Jews wherever he could. In response to the call from the *Judenrat*, Krupa hurried to the railroad station where the Jews were already boarding the deportation train. He informed the Gestapo that he needed 50 additional workers at his labor camp. The Gestapo gave him 50 Jewish men right there, at the railroad station. Among them were Mottel Gelbart and our friend Yechiel Lorent. Krupa himself led the 50 Jews from the station to *Judenrat* headquarters and handed them over to the *Judenrat*, explaining that he would send for them in two days. The *Judenrat* knew what to do. When Krupa returned two days later, the *Judenrat* did not give him the Jews (including Mottel) whom he had rescued at the railroad station, but 50 others who were clearly unfit for work. Krupa officially "accepted" them and then sent them home.

My neighbor Shlomo Schuman and his family are still in hiding at various Gentile homes.

The surviving Jews I meet are still in a state of shock. Nearly every one of them has lost relatives or friends in the *Aktion*. Wurst, the barber, who had taken shelter in the store of a Gentile neighbor, says he could hear the screams of the Jews seized next door and someone shouting, "Serves them right for killing Christ!"

Some Jews jumped from the deportation train. A few returned home but many more fell to their deaths or were shot by the Gestapo as they jumped. Others who escaped were caught by Gentiles who turned them over to the Gestapo.

Sokal, Sunday, September 20, 1942

Yom Kippur Eve. What will we eat to carry us over the fast tomorrow? I have managed to buy 10 decagrams (a little under a quarter-pound) of butter, but I am saving it for the children. Chana got a little dark bread and black coffee. This, plus a cucumber from my little vegetable patch, will be our meal before the fast. We have gone without food before, but this time we really want to fast for one full day.

Sokal, September 21, 1942

Yom Kippur is over. I said my prayers at home. Later, I went to my friend Shlomo Schuman, who has returned to his house with his family, and we talked about our bitter fate.

We have no food at home for breaking our fast. I hope that Shmelke can get us some food on his way home from work at the railroad.

Chaim stands at the door waiting for his Uncle Shmelke. It is already time for Shmelke to come by, but there is still no sign of him. I am getting worried. What could have happened to him?

A group of young men, friends of Shmelke, come to my door, They look frightened. They ask whether Shmelke is at my place. I reply that he isn't, and that I'm worried. They tell me that he left work together with them but then left them, explaining that he wanted to buy some food for us. The young men urge me not to worry; it may be another hour before Shmelke comes.

At last Shmelke arrives with a package under his arm. He is bruised and bleeding. "Shmelke! What happened to you?" I exclaim. He tells me that he lagged behind on the way home to buy us some food for breaking our fast. On Babiniec Street he was accosted by a Ukrainian policeman in a German uniform, walking with two girls. The Ukrainian, probably wanting to impress his girlfriends, yelled, "Jews! Stop!" The other workers, who had gone ahead of Shmelke, heard him but kept on walking. The Ukrainian grabbed Shmelke. "Why don't you raise your hat when you see a German uniform?" he shouted. "I'm sorry, I didn't see you," Shmelke replied. So the Ukrainian knocked him to the ground and kicked him several times with the heel of his boot. Shmelke dropped the package which contained our food.

Finally, the Ukrainian stopped kicking him. "Get up, Jew!" he yelled. When Shmelke didn't move, the Ukrainian roared, "Get up or I'll shoot you!" So, with the last of his strength, Shmelke got up. The Ukrainian and his two girlfriends walked away without another word. Shmelke picked up his package and dragged himself to my place.

In the package are a little bread and a few plums. That's the meal with which we break our Yom Kippur fast.

Sokal, September 24, 1942

I have received a postcard from my mother-in-law in Zolkiew telling me in prearranged code that she knew about the *Aktion* in Sokal, and that she went to the cemetery to pray for us at the graves of her grandparents. She was happy to hear that her prayers were answered. "I feel as if you had been born all over again," she writes.

• • •

The *Judenrat* has lost much of its former credibility. The Jews in Sokal no longer believe in it. The *Judenrat* has launched another fundraising drive, but nobody wants to give them any more money. The Jews say to the *Judenrat*, "Look, you managed to save your own skins in the *Aktion*, so you must have plenty of money stashed away somewhere. Why should we give you any more?" The Jews are calling the *Judenrat* by a new name: *Judenverrat*,* Jew traitors.

Dr. Steiner, the director of the *Judenrat*'s labor office, has disappeared. In fact, all the Jewish intelligentsia seems to be vanishing. Some of them have been arrested by the Gestapo; others were handed

---

* *Rat*: council; *Verrat*: treason.

Mrs. Halamajowa, her daughter Helen and the grandchildren. Helen's husband did not know of the family in the attic.

over to the Nazis by the local populace. Dr. Stolzenberg, a physician, has been arrested and shot for attempting to obtain forged "Aryan" documents for his daughter. Pessel, the pharmacist and former tax collector of the *Judenrat,* has been shot with his family. Moshe Kurtz, the local Jewish landowner, has been arrested along with his wife and daughter.

• • •

While I am visiting Shlomo Schuman, my son Chaim rushes in, shouting, "Father! Come home! Mama's crying and won't stop!" I run home. A Gentile driving through Sokal from Zolkiew has told Chana that her father died this week. He collapsed in the street. The cause of death was starvation.

• • •

I hear rumors at Schuman's tavern that a ghetto will be set up in Sokal. What are we going to do? I have very little cash left. I have stored up a little firewood and some potatoes for the winter, but what will happen now? A ghetto would mean certain death for us all.

I go to *Judenrat* headquarters and hear that the rumors about the ghetto are true. The *Judenrat* has already received orders from the Germans that all the Jews left in Sokal and Tartakov must move into the ghetto by October 15th. The boundaries of the area to be set aside for the ghetto will be determined by the *Judenrat* in cooperation with the Provincial Commissioner and the Gestapo.

Sokal, October 1, 1942

It is now Sukkoth, but what a sad holiday this year! The Jews are negotiating with the *Judenrat* for better housing in the ghetto. The *Judenrat* is already preparing additional apartments in the area set aside for the ghetto.

Mrs. Halamajowa comes to visit us. "I hear you'll have to move into a ghetto," she says. "Food is going to be scarce and expensive there. If you will give whatever belongings you can spare, I'll sell them and bring you food into the ghetto for the money.

• • •

According to Gestapo orders the ghetto area must be ready for occupancy by October 15th, and all Jews must move in by that date except for doctors and *Judenrat* members, who have until November 1st. The *Judenrat* people are busy in the part of town that has been marked out as the ghetto, measuring the housing space. Under the German ordinance two square meters of living space will be allowed for each person, but I hear that if you have good connections, you can get more.

• • •

I go to look for an apartment in the ghetto area. Old Mrs. Yachetz, who always lived in that neighborhood and therefore can stay right where she is, provided she does not take up more than the allotted living space, offers to let us move in with her. She could give us two tiny rooms in her apartment, subject to permission from the *Judenrat*. I like her apartment. I go to Abramche Schiffenbauer, head of the *Judenrat*'s housing office, who gives me a permit to move into Mrs. Yachetz's apartment with my wife and two children.

Sokal, October 6, 1942

My parents and Shmuel Letzter's family will move in with Abba Bilder, whose apartment, like that of Mrs. Yachetz, is in the ghetto. Letzter's former home outside the ghetto will be taken over by Zumbalski, the clerk of the municipal court. Zumbalski will have to move out of his own home because it is in the area assigned to the ghetto, where Gentiles, of course, will not be permitted to remain. Letzter and my parents would have liked to move into Zumbalski's former home but they can't have it because it has been requisitioned as headquarters for the Jewish police.

The *Judenrat* has enclosed the ghetto area with a barbed wire fence. The Gestapo comes every day to inspect the fence.

Sokal, October 11, 1942

Every day we move some more of our household into Mrs. Yachetz's place in the ghetto. We have sold off our good furniture long ago. All the furniture we have left is one iron bed, one bunk bed and a cradle for Lifshe. I'm also moving our reserves of firewood and potatoes into the ghetto.

IV

In the Ghetto, October–November, 1942

The Sokal Ghetto, October 14, 1942

This evening, Chana, our two children and I moved into our accursed new home in the ghetto.

The Sokal Ghetto, October 15, 1942

The ghetto was sealed this morning. The *Judenrat* has moved its headquarters from the former home of Hertz Konstantyn into the ghetto area. The *Judenrat* will operate from the house that once belonged to Rishe, the baker's widow.

The *Judenrat* is busy issuing identity cards for Jews employed in "official" positions.

The Sokal Ghetto, October 20, 1942

The *Judenrat* has received orders to add 25 men to the Jewish police. You must have either good connections, or good money, to be accepted into the Jewish police. These jobs are very much sought after because it is now generally believed that members of the Jewish police will be spared if there is an *Aktion*.

My brother Shmelke had a chance to become a ghetto policeman, but he did not accept the offer; he doesn't want to be labeled as a "collaborator" when the war is over.

• • •

Life in the ghetto is very hard. The squalor is beyond description—so many people confined to such a small space! There is a serious water shortage. The entire ghetto has only four wells. People are standing in line all morning for a little water. The pumps are breaking down from overuse.

Prices in the ghetto are three times what they are outside.

Every day additional Jews are brought into the Sokal ghetto from surrounding towns and villages, with just the clothes on their backs. They are placed into the worst apartments. Many families have been assigned living quarters that used to be stores, with brick floors and no cooking facilities. The present population of the ghetto is said to be 5,000, in a total area of two square kilometers.

The Germans are setting up labor camps outside the ghetto for skilled Jewish workers. The Jews assigned to work in these places have been ordered to spend the nights there instead of returning to the ghetto each evening. This arrangement has given rise to a rumor that there will be an *Aktion* in the ghetto one night soon. Now that the Jews are penned up in one single neighborhood, it will be easier for the Germans to arrest and deport them in larger numbers than it was when they were living dispersed in various parts of town. That is why the skilled workers will stay at their labor camps at night; if there is an *Aktion* during the night, these valuable tools in the German war effort will not be deported or killed along with the Jews in the ghetto. The Germans seem to be badly in need of skilled workers.

The Jews in the ghetto are in a state of panic each night because they don't know when the next *Aktion* will come. People are preparing bunkers and other hideouts beneath the ground floors and in the attics of their homes in the ghetto.

We go to *Judenrat* headquarters each evening to hear the latest news. My brother Shmelke has to answer constant questions about what the German workers at the railroad station tell of the world outside. People are passing rumors about the date of the next *Aktion.* Will it be the last *Aktion*? Perhaps there will be no more Jews left to kill when the next *Aktion* is over.

• • •

About 100 Jewish teenagers, boys and girls, have arrived in Sokal. They have escaped from Hrubieszow which they say is already *judenrein.* They have brought with them tools to open the railroad cars from the inside as they and others can escape if they are deported.

They tell us about the German atrocities against children, the old and sick in Hrubieszow. Everyone, alive or dead, was thrown into the boxcars of the deportation train.

• • •

People in the ghetto don't want families with little children to hide out in their bunkers during an *Aktion* because the crying of the children would give the hideout away to the Germans. Dr. Babad, a physician who was my classmate at *cheder*, tells me that women are asking him for sleeping pills to give their children to keep them quiet. But some of the children who take the pills never wake up again.

• • •

Mrs. Yachetz's place where we are now living is directly across the street from the new labor office of the *Judenrat*. Each morning the Jewish police bring to the labor office new workers whom they have dragged from their beds during the night. The members of the Jewish police are running through the ghetto like madmen, shouting at the top of their voices. You could almost think that an *Aktion*, not just an ordinary roundup for labor, is already going on. At first, I, too, panicked when I heard all this shouting in German, but now I can tell from the Yiddish accent and the bad grammar that the Germans aren't directly involved. For instance, the members of the Jewish police yell, *"Vu zennen die layt?"* (Where are the people?) If they were Germans, they would be shouting, *"Wo sind die Juden?"* (Where are the Jews?)

• • •

We have oil lamps, but the employees of the *Judenrat* have electricity in their homes.

The Sokal Ghetto, October 25, 1942

Perhaps I should place our baby Lifshe into a Gentile home to give her a chance of survival. She is only 14 months old, not yet able to talk. No one would ever know she is Jewish.

I obtain a special pass from my connections at the *Judenrat* so I can leave the ghetto for a few hours. I go to visit Mrs. Halamajowa. Her son happens to be there; he has come to visit his mother from the Strij area, where he manages an oil refinery for the Germans. He says he's seen what has been going on in the ghetto of the place where he lives.

I tell the Halamajowas that I think none of us Jewish adults will survive the war but that our children should have a chance to live. Would Mrs. Halamajowa be willing to take my baby daughter, Lifshe, into her home? Since Lifshe can't talk yet, her presence would not endanger the Halamajowas. No one would know she is Jewish. But if Lifshe survives this war, some memory, at least, will remain of our family. At first Mrs. Halamajowa refuses; she does not feel she can take this responsibility at her age. But when I plead with her to do it, and her son agrees, she says she will take Lifshe. I return to the ghetto in a happy mood. I tell my wife that I will take Lifshe to Mrs. Halamajowa the next morning. But Chana reports that Lifshe is sick. She seems to have an upset stomach. "I'd better keep her here for another few days," Chana says. Nevertheless, she starts to pack Lifshe's things.

The next day I write a letter addressed to a relative in the United States, my mother's brother Sam Suchman, who lives in Newark, New Jersey. I want him and his family to know that I have a little daughter named Lifshe and that I am about to place her into the home of a Polish Catholic woman, Mrs. Francisca Halamajowa, at No. 4 Street of Our Lady, in Sokal. I enclose a picture of Chana, Chaim and myself. I am doing this so that if Lifshe survives this war and grows up, she should know who her parents were and that she has family in the United States. I seal the letter and give it to Mrs. Halamajowa, telling her that I will bring Lifshe to her house in a few days and that she should keep the letter for Lifshe to read and to forward to America when she is old enough to understand.

As far as Chana, Chaim and I are concerned, we will seek shelter at the home of a Gentile in case there is an *Aktion*. But I am not quite sure where we should go. Lifshe is a baby who can't even talk as yet. But can I expect Mrs. Halamajowa to risk her life, and perhaps the lives of her son and daughter, by giving shelter to a Jewish couple and their six-year-old son? I am hoping that my brother Shmelke will be able to give us an early warning when the next *Aktion* comes, because he will see the deportation train being prepared in the station just as he did last time.

The Sokal Ghetto, Wednesday, October 28, 1942

I am awakened this morning by wild screams and heavy footsteps. At first I think it is the Jewish police again on their usual rounds to pick up Jews for forced labor. But this time the shouting and noise last longer than usual. I look out the window. I see that barbed wire fences have been strung up in the street at intervals of about ten meters. This is it: another *Aktion*. We get dressed quickly. I say to Chana, "Go hide with Chaim and Lifshe in one of the basement storage rooms. I'll run over to the Bilders and see what my parents and the rest of the family are going to do." The house in which we share the apartment with Mrs. Yachetz is large, with many apartments and many storage rooms in the basement. Chana and the children will find shelter in one of the storage rooms. I must take care of my parents.

The streets are filled with German and Ukrainian policemen in full fighting gear, complete with helmets and gas masks, as if they were going to the battlefront. Jews are scurrying about like poisoned mice in a trap. I also break into a run.

For a moment I think I should go back to Chana and the children, but by now I have almost reached Abba Bilder's house, where my parents, my sisters, my brother and the Letzters are living.

A German in uniform aims his rifle at me and shouts, "Halt!" but I keep running. Fortunately, he doesn't shoot.

I enter my parents' room. My father is there alone, in bed, coughing. He says that Mother, my sisters and Shmelke have gone down to the bunker which the Bilders have constructed in their cellar. Mother wanted to stay with Father, but he insisted that she go down to the bunker with the rest of the family. He told her he didn't feel well enough to be in a crowd. Besides, his constant coughing would lead the Germans to the bunker, whereas, if the Germans found only him in the room, they might look no further. Mother's duty was to save herself. "I am old and may not have much longer to live," he says to me. "But you children should have at least one parent left alive." I cannot answer Father's argument.

My father asks me whether I happen to have any money with me. I give him 200 zlotys. Perhaps the cash can persuade the murderers to leave him alone if they discover him in his room, and to believe him if he tells them that he is all alone in the house.

I rush to the cellar and demand to be let into the bunker. I want to see my mother and the others. Someone recognizes my voice and moves the trapdoor so I can enter. Crowded into a space of about three square meters are 25 people—men, women and children. My brother Shmelke is there; so are my sisters, all three of them, with little Feyge Chashe. My mother sits huddled in a corner. She seems to have aged 20 years since I last saw her only a few days ago. "He made me go. . . . Your father made me go and leave him in his bed. . . ." she says to me again and again. I can only shake my head and squeeze her hand.

The little children are the biggest problem in the bunker. They don't seem to understand what the excitement is all about.

The Sokal Ghetto, Thursday, October 29, 1942

At about 7:30 in the morning, we hear footsteps upstairs and a mixture of rough male voices, Yiddish and German. Is it the Germans, accompanied by the Jewish police? I hear one man ask my father in Yiddish, "Where is your family?" My father answers that he is all alone in the house. The others have already left for work. "Shmelke too?" the man asks. "Yes, Shmelke also," my father replies. (I recognize the man. He and Shmelke had gone to school together.) He adds that he won't let the Germans take him alive. They can shoot him in his bed. We wait with bated breath for the sound of a gunshot. What if the children in the bunker start to cry then? It would be the end for all of us.

I no longer hear my father asking to be shot. Perhaps he realizes the danger to everyone in the bunker if the cries of the children give us away.

A few minutes later we again hear heavy footsteps and excited voices conversing in Yiddish upstairs. "If we don't find the others, we're finished," says one of them. So it is the Jewish police! They have found my father and they will report him to the Germans. Will they also find the rest of us?

The Jewish police continues the search all through the house for another half-hour. Then we hear the men leave. Everyone in the bunker is relieved. Mother is crying softly. "Why can't I go with my husband?" she whimpers. At the moment I can think only of my wife and our two children. Where did they find shelter? But I must stay in the bunker and keep very quiet. I can't give the others away.

The children in the bunker begin to cry. They are hungry and thirsty and there is nothing for them to eat or drink. Someone offers a little boy a spoonful of liquid. The boy makes a face. "Tastes bitter," he complains. The man next to me takes a cube of sugar from his pocket and passes it to the child. "Here's some sugar. It won't taste so bitter now." Then he turns to me and says, "I saved this sugar for myself, but that little boy needs it more than I do." The bitter liquid that the little boy rejected, the man whispers in my ear, was urine.

We sit without moving and listen for sounds from upstairs. We don't know whether the *Aktion* is still continuing outside or whether the Germans have called it a day. I still hear my father coughing.

At about four o'clock in the afternoon, we hear voices upstairs, pure guttural German this time. We can hear my father's bed being dragged across the floor. Some men go down the steps; they seem to be carrying something heavy.

The search upstairs continues for about an hour. Then we hear someone saying in German with a strong Yiddish accent, "You see, sir, there's really no one else here. It was just that one old man." The footsteps and the voices grow distant. Apparently, the Germans and the Jewish police have left.

The Sokal Ghetto, Sunday evening, November 1, 1942

Our fourth day in the Bilder's cellar. At nine in the evening one of the women ventures outside. She returns and says it is safe for us to leave the cellar. But we decide to wait another night because the Germans may not be through with us yet. However, we hear nothing.

The Sokal Ghetto, Monday, November 2, 1942

Before dawn we again hear footsteps upstairs, but no voices this time. Someone cautiously raises the cellar trapdoor. People in civilian clothes, Poles, judging by their appearance—are looting the house. The *Aktion* must be over; if the Germans were still at work, no Gentile civilians would dare enter the ghetto. But we still stay where we are.

At daybreak we hear people conversing in Yiddish. The sound comes from the street. One of the men in our bunker goes out for a moment. He returns and tells us the *Aktion* is over. It is safe for us to leave. One by one, we emerge from the Bilders' cellar.

Mother, my brother, my sisters (Leah holding Feyge Chashe) and I go upstairs. Father is gone, and we are left to carry out his last wish: to survive so that we may keep the family together.

I part from the others and set forth for the Yachetzs' home to look for my wife and children. Other survivors are furtively making their way through the streets. People stop and inquire in whispers about each other's families. Bodies of Jews lying on the ground in pools of blood.

A man stops me and says my wife has already been at *Judenrat* headquarters twice to ask whether anyone has seen me. He says nothing about our two children. From this I conclude that I still have my wife but have lost my two children.

I wander through the streets trying to absorb that thought. What will my wife and I say to each other when we meet?

About an hour later, Chana comes stumbling toward me. I can hardly recognize her. She looks and acts as if she has gone out of her mind. She tells me that she has lost our children. We go to Mrs. Yachetz's building. Chana says the Germans and the Jewish police must have taken at least 150 Jews from there alone.

As we enter the courtyard, Mordechai, old Mrs. Yachetz's son-in-law, comes running. "We have your son Chaim!" Chana and I cannot believe it until we have reached Mrs. Yachetz's apartment and can touch and hug our son. Not a word is said about Lifshe.

Finally, Chana musters the strength to tell me her story:

After I left her to go to the Bilders', Chana grabbed Chaim by the hand, picked up Lifshe in her other arm and searched for a basement storage room in which to hide. They first went to the basement of Meir Berish, the owner of the building. That basement was already crowded. The people refused to let Chana in; they said the two little children would cry and the Germans would come and kill them all. When Chana begged for mercy, one woman yanked her by the hair and dragged her out the door.

Chana was ready to give up and meet death together with our children. But she remembered our resolve that we must not allow the Germans to wipe out our whole family. At least part of our family must survive. If this meant that we couldn't go into hiding together in one place, so be it.

Chana pushed Chaim into a woodshed in the courtyard. This woodshed was used for storing firewood and also, by some, as an outhouse. Chana piled firewood around Chaim to conceal him and gave him strict instructions to remain lying there quietly and not to make a move or sound until she would return to get him. Then, with Lifshe in her arms, she climbed the steps to the attic of the building. There was no other place left for her to go. If she and Lifshe were caught together in the attic, they would die together, but Chaim might remain undiscovered in the woodshed, so at least he would be spared.

Soon members of the Jewish police entered the building, searched it from top to bottom and took away virtually everyone.

The steps that led to the attic where Chana and Lifshe lay near a pile of old laundry were rickety, so the Germans stayed below and ordered the Jewish police to go up and search the attic for Jews. A Jewish policeman—his name was Joshua—discovered Chana and Lifshe. He covered them with a heavy blanket from the laundry pile and whispered to them to remain quietly under the blanket. Then he went downstairs and reported to the Germans that he had found no one in the attic.

But Lifshe began to cry. The Germans heard her and sent Joshua back to the attic. Joshua took Lifshe from Chana's arms. "Look," he whispered into Chana's ear. "The Germans have heard the baby. I can't tell them there's no one up here. They'd only kill me and send someone else to get the two of you."

"Then I'll go with Lifshe," Chana replied firmly. But Joshua shook his head. "No, you stay here," he said. "Perhaps you will survive and live to have other good Jewish babies." Once again, Chana remembered our decision; if there was an *Aktion*, we should not give the Germans the satisfaction of getting us all. Whoever in the family could save himself, should do so. Chana had to go on living for Chaim, and so she allowed Joshua to take Lifshe away. She herself lay quietly beneath the blanket all that day.

The next morning Chana pushed the blanket aside and, looking through a crack in the attic wall, saw Jews walking in the street. She reasoned that the *Aktion* must be over and she could go to the woodshed and get Chaim. But Chaim was not in the woodshed. Half-crazed with grief and horror, Chana raced through the streets of the ghetto to look for me. If I, too, had been killed, she would not care whether she herself lived or died. She went to *Judenrat* headquarters to ask whether I or anyone from my family had been seen at Konotopa Square, the assembly point where, the last time, the Jews had been gathered for deportation. When she was told that no one had seen me there, she felt faintly relieved. "Well, at least he hasn't been deported," she told herself. So she set out in the direction of the Bilders' house. Perhaps I might be there. And that is how Chana and I met in the street.

But how did our son Chaim survive? Chaim was able to tell his story quite coherently. From his hiding place behind the firewood in the woodshed, he saw the Germans chasing the Jews from the apartment building. Then he saw his sister Lifshe being carried in the arms of a Jewish policeman. Chaim's first impulse was to run after the man and grab Lifshe from him, but then he remembered what his mother had told him; not to make a move or a sound until she came back for him. So Chaim remained in the woodshed all day long without food or drink, and sick from the smell of excrement all around.

That evening, Mordechai, Mrs. Yachetz's son-in-law, passed the woodshed and heard a child moaning inside. He looked in and found Chaim there. He took him to his mother-in-law's apartment. There, Mrs. Yachetz, who had survived the *Aktion* in one of the storage basements, gave Chaim a little bread and water. And so Chana and I found at least one of our children alive.

I want to know what happened to my father in the end. I know now

that during the *Aktion* all the Jews seized by the Germans were assembled on Konotopa Square and ordered to squat on their knees. The
group was divided into two transports. The first was taken to the railroad station and herded into the boxcars at one o'clock in the afternoon; the second, at seven that evening. A total of 2,500 Jews from
Sokal, I am told, have been deported to the death camp of Belzec in
this *Aktion.*

Someone at *Judenrat* headquarters tells me he saw my father being
loaded into a boxcar together with eight other invalids. Other Jews in
the transport greeted him. *"Sholom Aleichem,* Reb Yossel, peace be
with you," they said. My father asked each person, "Did you see
anyone from my family on Konotopa Square?" When he was reassured
that no one of us had been seen at the assembly point, he said, "Good.
At least they won't be deported. Now just let Hitler and his gang go to
hell."

Others think that my father probably died before the cars of the
deportation train were sealed. Sick as he was, he may never even have
reached the station alive. The *Judenrat* workers are gathering up the
bodies of Jews who have perished in the ghetto during the *Aktion* and
are taking them to the cemetery for burial. The *Judenrat* informs my
brother Shmelke and me that the *shohet* (ritual slaughterer) and his two
sons will attend to the burial of the dead. Why don't we go to the
cemetery and see whether our father's body is there?

Shmelke and I set out for the cemetery, taking with us our father's
tallith and several wooden boards for a coffin, so we can give our
father a proper burial if we find him. As Shmelke and I walk to the
cemetery, some Poles run after us, shouting, "So there are still Jews
left in this town? Weren't they all put on the train?" We answer that
the Jews are still here.

In the cemetery, Shmelke and I look for our father's body among
the dead, but it is not there. We are surprised to see more than 20 un-
buried bodies. Some people in the cemetery say that the Germans put
many of the dead on a train to Belzec where the bodies will be turned
into soap.

Among the dead at the cemetery is the wife of Hersh Schlager. Her
head is missing. Hersh stands sobbing beside her body and tells us how
she died. When the Germans seized her, she offered them all her jewelry as they should spare her. The Nazis took the jewelry and then shot
her so that her head was severed from her body. Now Hersh is about to

bury what is left of her. Pesach Yachetz is there, too, waiting to bury his friend, a man by the name of Gashalter.

Since we haven't found our father, Shmelke and I are ready to leave the cemetery, but Pesach asks us to wait a while. He wants to get a *minyan** together so the Mourner's *Kaddish* can be recited aloud for all the dead after their burial. But it seems that Pesach will not be able to gather a *minyan* of ten survivors.

We see Notte Stanyatiner burying his infant grandchild. He tells us that he himself smothered the baby in the bunker so that its crying should not attract the attention of the Germans and endanger the lives of all the others.

Shmelke and I return to the ghetto.

The Sokal Ghetto, November, 1942.

The surviving Jews in the ghetto live in constant fear that, sooner or later, there will be another *Aktion*, the final one that will make Sokal *judenrein.*

A Gestapo man, dead drunk, has turned up at *Judenrat* headquarters, waving his gun. A little group of Jews are exchanging stories about the *Aktion.* What was this Gestapo man doing at *Judenrat* headquarters? The story is that several relatives of members of the Jewish police were rounded up in the *Aktion.* So one Jewish policeman came to the Gestapo man and asked him to have his relatives released. "I'll have your family released if you can get me 50 other Jews in exchange for them," said the Gestapo man. The Jewish policeman discovered a bunker full of Jews whom he handed over to the Gestapo man in exchange for a half-dozen members of his family.

The ghetto of Sokal is emptying out. Of the 4,000 Jews who originally moved into the ghetto, only 2,000 are left.

[*After the war I will hear from survivors that during this most recent* Aktion *a third transport left Sokal. That train stopped at Krystynopol and remained there for a long time. Krystynopol was an important railroad junction where the boxcars coming from Sokal were attached to sealed deportation cars from other localities to form one long train bound for Rawa Ruska. After that, the train made no other stops until it reached its destination.*

[*Among the deportees aboard that last train were Jews from*

---

* Prayer quorum of ten Jewish males above the age of 13.

Hrubieszow who had been caught in the ghetto of Sokal, including the young people who had so proudly shown me the tools with which they could open boxcars from the inside. When the train stopped at Krystynopol, they used their tools to unlock some of the cars, and Jews started to jump out. More than half the Jews from that transport jumped from the train. But only a few of the Jews from Sokal returned home alive. Some fell to their deaths as they jumped. Others were picked off by Gestapo snipers.

[Those few who returned described the mood of the Jews in the boxcars. They told, among others, the story of Mendale Melamed, a truly pious man, who calmly produced a bottle of brandy (no one knew where he could have gotten it) and drank a L'Chaim, a toast to life. "We ought to be happy," he explained, "because we will die as martyrs. Our souls will go straight up to heaven."

[My friend David Sturm, who survived the war, told me that he had some money with him. He distributed it among those who said they would try to jump from the train; he thought they might need it. Sturm also remembered a beer dealer by the name of Rosenberg, who pushed his way to the barred window of the boxcar looked out at the passing landscape and muttered, "Some wonderful world! You great, big wonderful world out there, you can kiss my ass!" Among those who refused to jump was a man by the name of Yoshe Elefant. "Why should I go through all that trouble?" he asked the others near him. "Just to remain alive so I can eat one more potato?"]

We see quite a few people in the streets of the ghetto with arms in slings and crude splints. These are the people who jumped from the boxcars and made it home to Sokal with broken bones, but alive. I meet a boy of 11, the son of a friend of mine. "Where is your mother?" I ask him. He answers that he was put on the deportation train with his mother and six-year-old brother. His mother and brother jumped from the train and were shot by the Germans. He jumped a few minutes later and ran past their bodies. The day after the *Aktion*, he returned to the ghetto, alone.

Mrs. Halamajowa and her son do a very brave thing. They enter the ghetto at the risk of their lives and come to see us at Mrs. Yachetz's apartment. They want to know why I didn't bring Lifshe to Mrs. Halamajowa's home as I said I would. When Chana and I tell her what happened to Lifshe, Mrs. Halamajowa bursts into a loud weeping and tears her hair. After she has calmed down, I say to her, "You can't help

Lifshe anymore. But perhaps you can help some of us others as you did once before. There will probably be another *Aktion* soon. This time the Germans will be out to get all the Jews. It's time for us to leave the ghetto. Could you allow part of our family to move into your hayloft and maybe give them a little food? If they can hide at your place, they may have a chance to survive this horror."

Mrs. Halamajowa says, "All right. I'll do it." I tell her that Chana, Chaim and my sisters Yitte and Chaye Dvora will move into her hayloft. I'll stay in the ghetto and find other hideouts for the rest of the family. My plan is to disperse the family in three separate hideouts so that there's a chance the Germans won't catch all of them.

My wife and two sisters begin to pack their most essential belongings and wait for the right time to leave the ghetto.

The Sokal Ghetto, November 3, 1942

Very early in the morning of November 3, 1942, when other Jews are leaving the ghetto for their work assignments, Chana, Chaim, Yitte and Chaye Dvora leave the ghetto to go into hiding. The grownups carry their usual safe-conduct passes stating that they have legitimate places of employment outside the ghetto. They keep about 200 meters' distance between one another in order not to attract attention. Six-year-old Chaim comes last, alone. He already knows the way. My brother Shmelke, who is going to work at the railroad station as usual, follows them at some distance to keep an eye on them.

The stationmaster, who formerly occupied half of Mrs. Halamajowa's house and wanted her to throw us out during the last *Aktion*, has moved away. A new tenant has moved in; a tax official with his wife, three daughters and an aged mother. He is a Polish liberal; in other words, not an anti-Semite.

This evening, on his way home from work, Shmelke stops at Mrs. Yachetz's apartment to tell me that my wife, my son and our two sisters Yitte and Chaye Dvora are now settled in the hayloft above Mrs. Halamajowa's pigsty.

The Sokal Ghetto, November 4, 1942

On his way from the railroad station, Shmelke takes some bedding to Mrs. Halamajowa's hayloft. He will take additional pillows, blankets and other such items each day until everything my wife, my son and our sisters need is at Mrs. Halamajowa's place. This time

Shmelke understands that no one, not even our Jewish friends, must know about our family's hideout. When Shmelke's friends, who go to work with him each morning, ask questions, they are told that Shmelke is taking the bedding to a Gentile woman so she can sell it for him and give him part of the money. Nowadays, such business transactions between Jews in the ghetto and Gentiles outside, though strictly illegal, are almost everyday occurrences.

I have left Mrs. Yachetz's place and moved in with my brother Shmelke and my sister Leah at the Bilders'. I have sold the little food, the firewood and the household goods I still had left. When people ask me questions, I do not tell them that my wife and son have gone into hiding. I say that I have lost my father and my little daughter in the *Aktion* and that the remaining family wants to live together. Apart from everything else, I explain, living together will help us save light and fuel.

No one in the ghetto sleeps at night anymore. We lie in our beds fully dressed. People are organizing groups to watch through the night for portents of an *Aktion*. Each night, other neighbors take on this guard duty. People are preparing new and better bunkers in which to hide. The next *Aktion* will be different from the previous two; the Nazi plan is that after this *Aktion* no Jews should be left alive in Sokal. So that *Aktion* will take longer than just a day or two and the bunkers in the ghetto have to be sufficiently secure to serve as hideouts for several weeks, or perhaps even months.

I feel a little relieved because part of my family is not at Mrs. Halamajowa's, outside the ghetto. This means I no longer have to worry about their immediate survival or about getting food for them.

The Sokal Ghetto, Mid-November, 1942

I have been talking with my brother Shmelke about hideouts for the rest of the family, not in ghetto bunkers, but at the homes of Gentiles. Shmelke, working at the railroad station, is looking for Gentile acquaintances from nearby villages who might be willing to give us help or advice.

One night I go to the suburb of Valevka, where my family owns a plot of land. A Jew who leaves the ghetto without special permission for any purpose other than going to his assigned work, is subject to the death penalty, but I don't let that stop me because my family and I have nothing to lose.

I set out at eight o'clock in the evening. I remove the Star of David from my coat sleeve, jump over the barbed wire fence and walk along the bank of the River Bug until I reach Valevka.

The farmer who lives next door to our piece of land is, I think, a decent man. I knock on his door. He himself answers. He is surprised to see me. "What are you doing here?" he asks. "I have a business proposition for you," I reply. "Come in," he says. It is warm and cheerful inside. He, his wife and their son are having supper. They offer me some food. It breaks my heart to see how some simple people in this world have all the comforts of life while others are dying of hunger and cold in the vale of tears from which I have just come, only 20 minutes' walk away.

I say to my host, "Hitler doesn't want any Jews to remain alive. But I do want to live and see him go down in defeat. Personally, I don't think Hitler can last much longer." Having said this, I make my offer. "As you know, my family owns several acres of land next to your fields. When this war is over, I will give you my land in perpetuity—no strings attached—if you will dig a bunker on your land where three people from my family can hide. You'll have nothing to do for them except to bring them a little food each evening, just enough to survive." I then tell him how the plan could be worked out. I also tell him that I'll have to go to see someone in Konotop, a village near Valevka, the next morning. I will take the ferry that transports workers and schoolchildren from Konotop across the River Bug to Sokal and then returns to Konotop virtually empty, before daylight. In this way I will not attract attention.

My host does not offer me a room in his house to spend the night but takes me into his stable to sleep on a pile of hay.

I remain awake all night, my teeth chattering from the cold.

The Sokal Ghetto, Mid-November, 1942

Early this morning I go to the bank of the River Bug to meet the Konotop-Sokal ferry. I have left my host without hearing from him whether he is willing to accept my offer. When I board the ferry, I freeze with fear because the boatsman turns out to be a man by the name of Cherkovsky, who used to work for my family and now has the reputation of being the most vicious anti-Semite in Konotop. However, Cherkovsky acts as if he is glad to see me, and ferries me across the river.

The man I want to see in Konotop is Joshka Bagorovitch, Mrs. Halamajowa's brother. He, too, worked for my family for some 20 years. He lives near the river. I knock on his door. He and his wife give me a friendly welcome. One of their four sons happens to be home on furlough from Germany. The Bagorovitches give me breakfast. After I have eaten I tell them that the Germans have taken my father and little daughter and that I am looking for a place where part of my family could hide out. I promise him that if he helps us and we survive the war, I will give him some land and a building I own in Sokal.

Bagorovitch suddenly acts rather distant. He says he doesn't want to get involved. I plead with him for about an hour but it doesn't help. Finally I say to him, "All right, I'll leave, But it is dangerous for a Jew to be seen outside the ghetto during the day. Could I stay in your attic until after dark? Then I can go back to Sokal." Bagorovitch says no. I have no other choice but to spend the night with the farmer in Valevka.

The Konotop-Sokal ferry returns and Cherkovsky takes me across. I offer him some money but he says he wants no money from me. He is only sorry that he has no bread or fat on the boat. If he did, he'd give it to me. When I get off the ferry, he says, "If you're still alive when this war is over, I hope we'll get together for a drink someday."

I spend the day in the Valevka farmer's stable. Not a word is said about my offer. After dark I return to Sokal and the ghetto. I squeeze through the barbed wire fence and soon am back in the room I share with my mother and Shmelke.

I report to Shmelke on the results of my efforts thus far. Shmelke also has some news, and it is not good. He has heard that a *Bezirkshauptmann*, a German district captain, has come to town from Kaminka. Sokal is part of that district. The *Bezirkshauptmann* is a Gestapo officer who searches the ghetto, house by house, and collects all the Jewish property still left after the *Aktion*, except, of course, the belongings of Jews working for the *Judenrat*. A warehouse for all these goods has been set up in a large building. The surviving Jews of Sokal are figuring out ways of protecting their last possessions. After all, they must have some belongings left to sell for cash or to barter for food so they can go on living.

You get up early in the morning, take your bedding and anything else you don't want to lose, hide it all in the cellar and cover it over with old rags so it shouldn't be "confiscated" during the day while you are away at work. At night, you bring everything back upstairs. But you can't carry your sticks of broken furniture downstairs and then back up again to your room each day. . . .

• • •

The Gestapo sends 100 horse-drawn wagons from neighboring villages into the ghetto to remove Jewish property. Actually, three wagons would be enough. There isn't that much Jewish property to be gotten from Sokal any more.

The Gestapo officer who supervises this operation is an older man with twisted features. The Jews call him *Shmatnik*, the rag man. He is escorted through the ghetto by a member of the *Judenrat* and some Jewish police. They drive from one street to another, enter the houses and clear out the few miserable belongings left by Jews who have been deported. But as a rule, the Jewish police stay outside while the Gestapo officer enters the buildings. When the Jewish police do enter an apartment and find the occupants still there, they leave without taking anything. The *Judenrat* does not want the Germans to confiscate too much Jewish property.

The search for Jewish property continues for two weeks. When the search is declared over, the Gestapo sends the *Judenrat* a bill in the amount of 10,000 zlotys for the use of 100 wagons!

The *Judenrat*'s warehouse is now filled to capacity with Jewish property that can be used as "gifts" for the Nazis. The Jews guard the warehouse day and night. The supervisor of the warehouse is a man by the name of Wolf Herold.

• • •

I visit a Jewish man to inquire about a Gentile at whose home I could hide out. But I make my inquiries in such a way that the Jewish fellow shouldn't suspect that I want to go into hiding.

When I get to his house, I find several other people already there, discussing the subject Jews talk about these days: *Aktionen* (past and future) and who has survived the last *Aktion*. One man tells how, during the *Aktion* just past, he lay hidden in a hayloft with 40 other Jews. The *Schupo** came in, accompanied by Wolf Herold. The *Schupo* men sent Herold up to the hayloft to see whether any Jews were hidden there. Herold went up and returned to report that he had found no Jews. All these 40 Jews, plus the man who told the story, survived the *Aktion*.

---

* Nazi security police.

After a while I leave. As I pass through the street of our *Beth Medrash*, I hear a shot and see a Jew running. It takes me some time to find out what happened. It seems that *Shmatnik*, the Gestapo man, came to make his routine inspection of the *Judenrat* warehouse and shouted at Wold Herold that some goods which he, *Shmatnik*, had personally confiscated from Jews was missing. "Where's the stuff?" he demanded. Herold explained that the goods had been removed by local Gestapo men. *Shmatnik* worked himself into a towering rage. "Why did you let them take those things?" he bellowed. "How could I have kept the Gestapo men from taking them?" Herold asked. Thereupon *Shmatnik* pulled out his gun and pumped a bullet into Wolf Herold. That's the same *Shmatnik* of whom some Jews have been saying, just recently, that he isn't so bad. . . .

• • •

The Sokal Ghetto, end of November, 1942

The newspapers in Lvov have announced that Sokal will not be made *judenrein* after all; it will become a *Judenstadt*.* This means that when Jews have been cleared out from all other towns, the ghetto in Sokal will be maintained to accept Jews who have been expelled from neighboring localities—a solitary island in a sea of blood.

Jews are beginning to arrive in the Sokal ghetto from Wolyn province. For months these people have been wandering through the woods or hiding out at the homes of Gentiles. Now they have heard that while deportations of Jews from Sokal will continue, the town will not be made *judenrein*, so they think they have at least a chance of survival if they move into the Sokal ghetto. They have to enter the ghetto secretly because the *Judenrat* is not permitted to admit Jewish "fugitives" on its own authority. But the *Judenrat* is turning a blind eye to what is happening.

The Germans are bringing Jews from Radziew, Stojanew, Witkow and Tartakow into the Sokal ghetto. They notify the Jews that they will be transferred to the ghetto in Sokal and that they will be allowed to take their belongings with them. So the Jews remove their belongings from the various places where they have put them for safekeeping, pack them up and climb into wagons driven and escorted by Gestapo men. But the wagons make a stop at the *Judenrat* warehouse, and the

---

* Literally, "Jew-Town."

Gestapo men remove the baggage from the wagons and carry it inside, leaving the Jews in the wagons without possessions, barefoot and virtually naked. Then the wagons proceed through the snow to the ghetto houses, where the Jewish police is waiting for the newcomers.

The newcomers are crowded into cold, filthy tenements without stoves. The families are living literally one on top of the other. That is how the population of the Sokal ghetto has grown to 5,000 again; of these, only 40 percent originally lived in Sokal.

The misery of the newcomers is indescribable. People who were once in comfortable circumstances are now paupers, stumbling through ghetto streets with little pots, begging for a drop of soup. Women who have lost their families are wandering through the ghetto as if in a trance. One woman runs around screaming, "Where is my husband? Where are my children?"

But the saddest development is the total disintegration of morals. Men who were happily married for many years and then lost their wives and children in an *Aktion*, pick up young girls who have also lost their families. They take the girls to live with them and give them the clothes of their departed wives. One professional man I know has moved in with a woman for no other reason but that she has a halfway habitable apartment and a small reserve of food. Marriages do take place, but most of the unattached men and women don't bother with a wedding ceremony. Girls from cultured, prominent Jewish families are keeping company with men from the Jewish police who are real scum. The girls think that if they play up to these yokels they will be able to survive.

There is a tavern in the ghetto, complete with entertainment, where these types go. It is at the home of Wolf Chayim, the son of Joshua Moshe. The entertainment is directed by Itche Petroczyner, a deputy chief of the Jewish police. That's where the members of the Jewish police hang out with their girlfriends and buy the best of everything with money left behind by the deportees whom they helped seize in the *Aktion*. Other guests are just ordinary Jews with a little money to spend, who want to fill their stomachs with food before they die, rather than let the Nazi murderers have all the money.

• • •

I spend a lot of time walking through the ghetto streets and visiting friends to hear reports of what is happening in the world outside and on the battlefronts.

I visit my former neighbor, Shlomo Schuman. His wife, Altshe, has a heart of gold. She shares every bit of food in her house with the poor who have nothing. The Schumans are among the very few who know that my family has gone into hiding. But they think I was crazy to let them do that. They say you can't ever trust a Gentile.

I also go to see Mottel Gelbart, Shmuel Letzter's son-in-law, who is now living at the home of Abraham Chaim, where all the *Judenrat* people gather and exchange the latest news. Abraham Chaim still runs his little grocery store as he did before the war despite the desperate shortage of food. Sometimes he even has a little tobacco to sell. Also, he receives packages of raisins and almonds from his children, who are living in Italy. Whoever still has the money can buy them.

I have told Mottel about my plan to find hiding places for the rest of my family, who are not in Mrs. Halamajowa's hayloft. Like the Schumans, Mottel doesn't think it's a good idea, but I don't care how others feel about it. I keep figuring out possibilities of smuggling the rest of my family, and myself, out of the ghetto.

• • •

One evening panic breaks out in the ghetto. Is another *Aktion* imminent? I take off my armband with the Star of David, cross the barbed wire fence under cover of darkness, and am off to Valevka, to the house of the farmer to whom I have promised my family's land adjacent to his, if he builds me a bunker in which we can hide.

Shlomo Schuman and his wife, perished in the second action.

I knock on his door. He lets me in and gives me some supper. I take him aside and repeat my proposition to him. Has he come to a decision? I ask. "No, Moshko," he replies. "It's out of the question. I'm scared. If the punishment for giving shelter to Jews would be no more than a small fine, I'd take the chance and help you. But frankly, I don't want to put my life on the line for you."

I try to talk him into reconsidering his decision, but to no avail. He graciously permits me to spend the night in his stable again.

At about midnight, I hear a commotion in the courtyard. Then I hear the door of the barn open. My host is bringing some people into his barn. I recognize their voices. They are Yossel Rechtol, a member of Sokal's Jewish police, and his wife and children. It seems that Yossel wants to have his family hide out in the barn if there is an *Aktion.* It turns out that this is a prearranged deal. My host has been in touch with Rechtol all along. Apparently this Gentile is willing to risk his life for Jews after all, if the price is right.

I spend a sleepless night. I am afraid there will be an *Aktion* in Sokal the next day. If a member of the *Judenrat's* police is ready to hide his family outside the ghetto, it must mean he knows that an *Aktion* is imminent.

In the morning I listen for gunfire from the direction of the Sokal ghetto, but I hear nothing. The farmer's wife enters the stable with some breakfast for me. I ask her whether she has heard of anything unusual going on in the Sokal ghetto. She answers that all seems to be quiet there. Nevertheless, that morning, her husband takes Yossel Rechtol's wife and children into his barn.

I stay in the stable all that day. From time to time I look out through a crack in the wall. I see a few Gentiles I know. Some are headed in the direction of the woods; others are going to work in the fields near here. I don't dare go back to Sokal.

• • •

After dark I go to see an elderly Gentile couple who are living near Valevka. The man is making reins for wagon horses. Perhaps I'll be able to make an arrangement with them.

When I arrive at their home, a scruffy dog hurls himself at me, ready to tear me to pieces. Luckily the old man comes out just in time to drag the beast off me. He invites me to come inside. I ask him whether I can spend the night at his place. This, I think, will give me an opportunity to discuss my problems with him. But he refuses to let me stay. "Ask Zdenko, the man who lives next to that plot of land you own." But Zdenko is the farmer who just turned me down in favor of Yossel Rechtol and his family.

I slowly walk away. I am stunned. So things have reached a point where not even a nonentity like this old reinmaker is willing to give me shelter for the night.

As I walk alongside the bank of the River Bug, I hear footsteps behind me. I hide behind some bushes. The steps come closer. It is Yossel Rechtol. I stop him and ask him what is going on in the Sokal ghetto. He says that all is well. It sounds like a soldier making a battle report to his superior. "Begging your leave, sir, there's three dead and three wounded. All is well." But Yossel tells me that his deal with Zdenko is off. He is returning to Zdenko's place to take his wife and children back to the ghetto.

• • •

Back in the ghetto, I continue my search for a hideout. My brother Shmelke reports that he met a Gentile acquaintance at the railroad station. This man is living in the countryside near Sokal and says he would be willing to take me into his home.

• • •

The latest news is that Janowszinski, the chairman of the *Judenrat*, has disappeared. When he failed to show up at his office, members of the Jewish police went to his home to look for him. They found the house padlocked. His old mother is still in the ghetto but neither she nor anyone else seems to know where Janowszinski is. There are rumors that he has fled by plane to neutral Switzerland, taking with him a large amount of cash from the *Judenrat* treasury.

Janowszinski's disappearance is a bad sign because he was in close touch with the Gestapo. Perhaps things will become even worse for the Jews in Sokal and he knew about it.

The *Judenrat* needs a new chairman. The most popular candidate is Dr. David Kindler, a general practitioner and gynecologist who has been active in Sokal's Jewish community for many years, working for philanthropic causes and for the Zionist movement. But Dr. Kindler has declined the honor. He says he doesn't want to be the head of an organization he considers little better than a gang of chickenhearted collaborators.

The second choice is Schwartz, the engineer who was once in charge of our soup kitchen. An active member of the Revisionist

Zionist party,* he served as the last elected chairman of Sokal's Jewish community before the war. Schwartz doesn't want the *Judenrat* job either, but the Germans have told him that if he doesn't accept, he will be reported to the Gestapo. So Schwartz has no other choice but to accept and he is now the chairman of the *Judenrat.*

• • •

Early one morning, my friend Chaim Levogy and I accompany my brother Shmelke to his job at the railroad station. Shmayale, a member of the Jewish police, stops us on the way. "Where are you working, Maltz?" he wants to know. I tell him I am working for Zulchinski, the cattle dealer and wholesale butcher. "That's no real job," says Shmayale. "Come with me." He takes me to the labor office of the *Judenrat.* It seems that additional workers have been requisitioned for the *Judenrat* warehouse. Working at this warehouse is not a pleasant job. That's where Wolf Herold was shot.

I am told to wait until a whole group of workers has been assembled; then we'll be marched off to the warehouse together. I look around the labor office for friends who could get me out of this mess. I go up to one of the bigwigs, Itshe Gleicher. "Let me off," I say to him. Gleicher says he can't do that. I go to another big shot, Azriel Unger. Unger won't look me straight in the face. No hope there, either.

After a while, four additional Jews are brought in and we set out for the warehouse. On the way I say to one of the other men, "I'll be back. I'll just go buy a loaf of bread." But instead of going for bread, I quickly turn into a side street. I make it to Shlomo Schuman's place. It's still early in the morning, so I wash myself and recite the morning prayers. Then the Schuman's give me breakfast.

Suddenly my mother comes rushing in. "Is my son Moishe here?" she cries, too upset to say more. After I have calmed her down, she tells me that the Jewish police has been looking for me. I tell her not to worry. I stay with the Schumans' until noon. Then I go home to my mother.

• • •

This incident, following so closely on Janowszinski's disap-

---

* The right-wing, activist Zionist party founded by Vladimir Jabotinski. Among the best-known products of this party is Israel's Polish-born former prime minister, Menahem Begin.

pearance, has convinced me that I must leave the ghetto at once. My plan is to go to the town of Opolsk, where I know a Ukrainian who I hope will give me shelter. But before I go there, I want to spend a few days with my wife, my son and my two sisters in Mrs. Halamajowa's hayloft to make sure that won't go cold or hungry.

Shmelke and I agree that he will pick me up from Mrs. Halamajowa's house on his way home from work next Friday evening, November 27, and escort me to Opolsk.

V

In the Hayloft

Late November, 1942

When I arrive at Mrs. Halamajowa's house to visit my family, she says she cannot take me up to the hayloft because it is already bright daylight and I mustn't attract attention to the pigsty. She takes me into the cellar of her home to wait until dark. She apologizes for not letting me wait in her living room. She has five young Gentile students as boarders, plus two girls living with her. The girls, she explains, are related to her daughter-in-law. These people must not see me.

[*Later I learn that the two girls were not Gentiles but Jewish, the daughters of an engineer for whom Mrs. Halamajowa's son once worked.*]

I sit in Mrs. Halamajowa's cellar all day long. She gives me several written messages to take up to my family when I go to them in the hayloft after dark, and she asks me to bring back written replies when I leave. She does not want to visit her "lodgers" in the hayloft too frequently, for fear that the boarders in her house may discover that she is giving shelter to Jews.

At noon, Mrs. Halamajowa brings me lunch in the cellar. I take her into my confidence. I ask her whether I could stay with my family in her hayloft for just a few days. After that I will go to a Ukrainian in Opolsk and ask him to take me into his home. "Don't go to that man," Mrs. Halamajowa says when I tell her his name. "He'll kill you. It would be better for you to move into my hayloft and stay with your family."

That evening she takes me to her pigsty, which is adjacent to her house, and guides me up a ladder to the hayloft. Now there are five of us in Mrs. Halamajowa's hayloft, a space as big as one middle-sized room with a very low ceiling: my wife, my two sisters, Yitte and Chaye Dvora and myself. Chaye Dvora is in a very rundown condition due to the hardships she had endured. During the fierce winter of 1941–42 she did slave labor as a housemaid for a Ukrainian family.

Early the next morning, I hear the door of the pigsty creak open. It was Mrs. Halamajowa with a pot of soup, which she carries up the ladder to our hayloft. It is not like any soup I ever ate in the ghetto. At noon she brings us lunch. Her food is very tasty.

After the meal, I get a few hours' sleep. Afterwards, I inform Mrs. Halamajowa that I have decided to accept her offer. I won't go to Opolsk but will move into her hayloft. She says she is glad I have made up my mind to stay.

That Friday night, November 27, when Shmelke comes to pick me up, I tell him that I won't go to Opolsk but have decided to move into Mrs. Halamajowa's hayloft. But first I want to go back to the ghetto to see what to do with our mother, my older sister Leah and Leah's little girl, Feyge Chashe, who is three-and-a-half years old.

It is snowing when Shmelke and I pass through the ghetto gate. We see Jews who, we are told, just arrived in Sokal from the town of Radziew, which has been made *judenrein*. Some of them have little children. They are soaked to the skin and shivering with cold. I see Itshe Gleicher and his brother, the big shots from the *Judenrat*, standing nearby. Where will the *Judenrat* find rooms for these new arrivals?

When Shmelke and I arrive at the Bilder's home where our mother and Leah are staying, we find Leah sick in bed. The doctor has been there; he said she had typhoid fever.

An hour later, hysteria breaks out in the ghetto again. There is a rumor that someone in the ghetto has received a telegram from relatives in Lvov, saying, "Auntie will come to visit you soon." This is the prearranged code indicating that another *Aktion* can be expected in Sokal any day.

Jews are huddling together in the streets with fear on their faces. "What's the latest?" they ask each other. It is 11 o'clock at night, but the ghetto is a beehive. People are scurrying through the snow-blanketed streets, taking their belongings to bunkers they have built in the ghetto.

"Why don't you also move into Mrs. Halamajowa's hayloft?" I ask Shmelke. "Why live in constant fear when we have such a good hideout?" Shmelke and I agree that he will bring our mother to the hayloft with him. We'll leave Leah and Feyge Chasha at the Bilder's house with Leah's father-in-law until she has recovered.

That very night Shmelke, our mother and I leave the ghetto at an unpatrolled spot and walk along the bank of the River Bug, following Mrs. Halamajowa's directions how to get to her pigsty without being noticed. We pass the church she has pointed out to us as a landmark, and then we look for her backyard. We pass several backyards before we finally find hers. The three of us enter the pigsty and climb up the ladder to the hayloft, but the door to the hayloft is locked from the outside. Shmelke goes out on his tiptoes and knocks on Mrs. Halamajowa's bedroom window. She gets up, climbs the ladder, unlocks the hayloft door to let us in, and then locks the door again behind us.

The next morning, Mrs. Halamajowa says that nothing new has happened in the ghetto. The rumor that the *Aktion* was apparently a false alarm. Shmelke and I decide that he should go to work at the railroad as usual and then return to the Bilder's home in the ghetto to be with our sister Leah. Eventually the family will be split up in accordance with my original plan that the Germans should not be able to take all of us together, and also in order not to endanger Mrs. Halamajowa's life (and our own lives) by overcrowding the hayloft unless something drastic happens in the ghetto. Shmelke will stay in the ghetto for the present but move in with us when he thinks the time has come.

So Shmelke bids us good-bye and leaves for his job on the railroad. Mother is staying with us in Mrs. Halamajowa's hayloft. Shmelke will be back in a few days' time to escort her back to the ghetto where she can look after Leah and Feyge Chashe.

• • •

Two days later, Shmelke stops at Mrs. Halamajowa's after work and takes Mother home with him. I stay in the hayloft with my wife, my son and my two sisters, Yitte and Chaye Dvora, making a total of four adults and one child hidden in the hayloft above Mrs. Halamajowa's pigsty.

At this point, I should describe Mrs. Halamajowa's setup. Half of the house in which she lives belongs to her; the other half belongs to her neighbor, a man by the name of Benerowicz. Behind the house there is a backyard—better, a garden—that extends all the way down to the bank of the River Bug. The pigsty with its hayloft is, as I have already said, a separate building. The hayloft is separated from the attic of Mrs. Halamajowa's house by a partition of boards. Mrs. Halamajowa has sole use of the hayloft and of half the attic. There are no toilets in Mrs. Halamajowa's house, so she and her neighbors and boarders use an outhouse in the pigsty. We are locked up in the hayloft all day and all night, so that no one who enters the pigsty should see us. The only light we get is the bit of daylight that can seep in through cracks in the wall of the hayloft.

In the hayloft, December, 1942

We have screened off part of our hayloft with a cotton sheet. This is our private toilet since, of course, we cannot go down to use the outhouse in the pigsty. We use a bucket behind the cotton sheet and whoever needs it, uses it. Mrs. Halamajowa takes the bucket downstairs each day, empties it and brings it back to us fresh and clean. She has bought three squealing piglets and ten chickens, not only for food (eventually) and eggs, but also that the neighbors should not become suspicious when they see her carry pots or bowls of food from her house to the pigsty. When she pours the slop from our bucket, she mixes it with the slop form the pigs, again to keep the neighbors and her own boarders from becoming too nosy. So the piglets and the chickens have an important function: they help keep the neighbors and Mrs. Halamajowa's boarders from finding out that Mrs. Halamajowa, who speaks a perfect German and proudly recalls the years she spent in Germany, is giving shelter to Jews.

In the morning Mrs. Halamajowa's neighbors and boarders all troop into the pigsty to use the outhouse. It's a great commotion. We listen with bated breath to be sure they are gone before we start moving around in our hayloft. We don't want anyone to hear us. We've developed this operation to a fine art. The young students who board with Mrs. Halamajowa don't take too long to do their business in the outhouse, and when they leave, they slam the door so we know exactly when it is safe for us to move. But the older people, Mrs. Halamajowa's neighbors, take a little longer and close the door more gently when they leave. So we have to strain our ears to hear whether they have left or are still occupying the outhouse. If it snows during the night, the snow on the ground muffles the footsteps of all the people when they pass through the backyard between Mrs. Halamajowa's house and the pigsty, making it even more difficult for us.

• • •

On December 6, St. Nicholas' Day, Mrs. Halamajowa's daughter Hela comes to visit, with toys and candy she has bought especially for

Halamajowa and her daughter Hela, 1960.

Chaim.* Hela actually treats us like human beings; she seems to have a special feeling for children. And just about one kilometer from the Halamajowa home there is a ghetto, where Jewish children suffer from hunger, cold and abuse.

• • •

Back in Sokal, Shmelke goes to his job on the railroad every morning. On their way to work, Shmelke and his friends pass Mrs. Halamajowa's backyard. Sometimes they see her there, drawing water from her well. She stops and asks them with a note of good-humored banter in her voice, "Hello, there, Jews! Are you still alive?" Sometimes Shmelke slips a message for us into her hand—quickly and surreptitiously, so his friends shouldn't notice. They must not know that Shmelke's family has gone into hiding, and where. All they know is that Shmelke is transacting some kind of business with Mrs.

* St. Nicholas' Day is celebrated in many European countries as a prelude to the Christmas season. Good boys and girls receive candy and little toys from St. Nicholas as a foretaste of the bigger gifts which the "Christ Child" will leave under their Christmas tree later in the month. Naughty children get only birch switches as a reminder of the whipping they deserve.

Halamajowa. They warn Shmelke that this woman is a dangerous anti-Semite. Shmelke doesn't answer them.

Shmelke's notes give us the latest news from the ghetto. Each report is worse than the one that has come before. Hunger and misery are rampant; hardly a day passes without deaths from starvation or disease.

Seemann, the Gestapo hero who shot Efraim Windler, has come to the ghetto. He saw my friend Moshe Weber in the street and shot him on the spot. It seems that Seemann had recognized Moshe as one of the people who had jumped from the deportation train. Then Seemann walked away, leaving Weber's body lying on the sidewalk. Abish Veta's daughter and her family escaped from the slaughter in the town of Most, only to be seized and shot as they entered the Sokal ghetto.

• • •

The winter is getting worse; it is bitter cold in our hayloft. Mrs. Halamajowa has given us four pairs of warm boots. We lie in the hay all day long, covered with blankets Shmelke has brought us from our home. When we awake in the morning, the blankets are covered with a thin sheet of ice. When it snows, the floor of the hayloft is soon covered with snow that comes in through the cracks in the wooden wall. We lie still, listening for people entering or leaving the outhouse in the pigsty. Sometimes we only hear a person leaving; we haven't heard him enter because the ground outside is blanketed with snow. We worry all day long whether anyone in the house might have heard us moving about in the hayloft.

From time to time, Shmelke brings Mrs. Halamajowa some bread and butter to help feed us. A woman who sells newspapers, delivers Polish and German dailies to Mrs. Halamajowa every afternoon. One of the newspapers is *Das Reich*, the personal mouthpiece of Joseph Goebbels, Hitler's minister of propaganda. When Mrs. Halamajowa is finished with the papers, she brings them up to us. But we have to wait until the next morning to read them, for by the time we receive them it is dark outside and there is no more light in the hayloft. In the morning I put on my winter wraps, including warm gloves, so I can stand close to a crack in the wall through which a sliver of winter daylight enters the hideout along with the icy December blasts. That's where I read the newspapers from the preceding day.

• • •

The Christmas holidays are coming. The Gentile students who are boarding with Mrs. Halamajowa have gone home for the holidays, but her neighbor's daughters have arrived from Lvov with their boyfriends. One of these young men isn't too much of a problem because he sings all the time so we can always tell where he is and behave accordingly.

• • •

On December 23, Mrs. Halamajowa's son arrives with his wife and four German friends. The son has brought with him holiday delicacies which he bought as he passed through Lvov. He has remembered the unfortunate people in his mother's hayloft; he has brought us a box of cookies, one whole salami and several bottles of beer. We haven't seen, much less eaten, such delights in a long time.

• • •

After Christmas Mrs. Halamajowa brings her son to visit us in the hayloft. "Aren't you freezing up here?" he asks. I immediately protest, "No." We all insist that we are happy and comfortable so we should not have any trouble with Mrs. Halamajowa or her children. Young Halamajowa tells us news you don't get to read in the German newspapers. He reassures us that Hitler and this war can't last much longer.

In the hayloft, January, 1943

Mrs. Halamajowa.

After her son has left, Mrs. Halamajowa comes up to the hayloft and asks me what I intend to do since there has been no *Aktion* in the ghetto. Do I want to stay on in her hayloft, or would I prefer to return to the ghetto? If my family and I want to stay, I should tell her now. In that case she will ask her boarders to leave because they and we together would be too much work and worry for her.

I immediately answer that all five of us—my wife, my son, my two sisters and I—would like to stay. I promise Mrs. Halamajowa that if, with God's help (and hers), we survive this war, I will buy the other half of her house and give it to her as a gift so she will be the sole owner of the house in which she lives. She laughs in sheer delight because she would like that very much.

• • •

When Mrs. Halamajowa brings us the German newspaper, the first thing I look for is the *Wehrmacht* communiqué, which is always on the front page. One day there are triumphant reports about British ships destroyed, and British and American planes shot down over Germany. But the news from the Russian front sounds quite different. I read that Hitler's forces have broken out from a Russian trap near Leningrad and have taken many Russian prisoners. In the Stalingrad sector to the south, the German Sixth Army, under the command of General Paulus, is surrounded by Russian forces but is putting up a heroic fight to break through the Red encirclement. I am surprised that Hitler should allow the German press to admit that one of his armies has been trapped by the enemy. This is a big change from his former boasts; so the tide of battle must be turning.

• • •

My heart is filled with new hope. Perhaps we will be able to survive until it's all over. General Paulus and his Sixth Army have surrendered to the Russians on Hitler's personal orders! Paulus has received the highest German military decoration in absentia. A period of mourning has been ordered for the entire Reich and all German-occupied territories. All places of amusement will be closed for four days.

• • •

Mrs. Halamajowa has brought me a note that Shmelke dropped off on his way to work. It says that the Jews of the ghetto of Sokal are as well and content as can be expected under the circumstances. [*But later we hear that Jews, even then, were being killed in Rawa Ruska. That city, to the southwest of Sokal, once had 12,000 Jews. Almost 80 percent of them originally came from other localities. They jumped from the deportation trains bound for Belzec. The Jews of Rawa Ruska had no illusions about Belzec. Since Belzec is only 20 kilometers from their city, the Jews of Rawa Ruska knew exactly what Belzec was all about.*]

These reports of Jews being murdered are especially heartbreaking now when it is clear that Hitler cannot win this war.

There are rumors that all the Jews in the Sokal ghetto will have to assemble on the square near the *Beth Midrash* on Monday, January 18, for inspection by the Gestapo. Jews dread these inspections because they know from past experience how these affairs always end.

Despite the knee-high snow, Shmelke has brought our mother, our sister Leah (who is still sick) and Leah's daughter, Feyge Chashe to Mrs. Halamajowa's hayloft. The four of them arrive at our hideout (Shmelke carrying Leah on his shoulders) in the middle of the night. We make up a bedstead of sorts for Leah. Typhiod fever usually takes up to eight weeks to run its course. We inform Mrs. Halamajowa that our sister is sick and needs good food. Mrs. Halamajowa even offers to take her into her own home and to give her a good bed, but I gratefully decline because I am afraid the Germans will discover all of us then.

Mrs. Halamajowa brings Leah good food every day. Leah's little daughter, Feyge Chashe is three-and-a-half years old and doesn't like her new home. She wakes up crying each night. We decide to send her back to the ghetto, to her grandfather, Shmuel Letzter, who still lives with the Bilders, because we are afraid that her crying will give us away to the Germans. When Shmelke passes by on his way from work that very evening, he comes up to the hayloft, picks up our little niece, and takes her back to the ghetto.

When January 18 passes without a sign of an *Aktion*, my mother and Leah also return to the ghetto. We have decided once again to disperse the family, this time primarily because we want to make things as easy as possible for Mrs. Halamajowa. If I left and returned to the ghetto, she could save another Jew in my place. She wouldn't care who it was, as long as it means saving another innocent life. That seems to be almost a religion with her. Instead, I am here, in her hayloft, taking up the place of some other Jew who could be sheltered here.

But I have no illusions about the situation in Sokal. No matter what they say about setting Sokal aside as a *Judenstadt*, the Germans will decide one day to have a final *Aktion* to make Sokal *judenrein*. In that case, we would certainly need a place where we can take shelter.

Shmelke has written to me what Mottel Gelbart is saying about us. Mottel thinks that either I should return to the ghetto, or else the whole family, including myself, should leave the ghetto together and go into hiding, somewhere in the "Aryan" sector, because if some Jewish informer inside the ghetto reports any one of us to the Gestapo, the entire family is as good as dead.

I am afraid that if the Germans decide to make Sokal *judenrein,* Mrs. Halamajowa may panic and put us out. So I think we should have a hideout on reserve also inside the ghetto, to use if this happens.

Shmelke writes that the people are beginning to notice my absence. They guess the reason and have been asking Shmelke to find a hideout for them—"the kind your brother must have found. Money is no object."

Among those who have approached Shmelke is Dr. David Kindler, the doctor who refused the chairmanship of the *Judenrat.* We've always had a good relationship with Dr. Kindler. One Sabbath in the 1930s, when Shmelke got a fishbone stuck in his throat, our parents took him to Kindler, who removed the bone. Kindler also once treated our father for a sprained foot. Of course, we always paid him well for his services, but he was a very devoted friend and Shmelke wants to help him. In addition to his gynecological and general practice, Kindler worked as a doctor for the railroad before the war. Perhaps, Kindler suggests, some railroad employee will remember him and give shelter to him and his family.

Dr. Kindler had been doing a lot to help the Jews in the ghetto. He visits the sick free of charge and his wife prepares food for the poor.

Mrs. Kindler and Dr. Kindler standing at left, Ebelsberg, Austria.

Shmelke has begun to talk to various Poles at the railroad about helping Dr. Kindler, but it seems that nobody wants to risk his life by giving shelter to the Kindlers.

Dr. Kindler has asked Shmelke to see whether the older of his two sons, Sever (we prefer to call him by his Hebrew name, Simcha), a boy of 14, could get a job at the railroad station. In this way, Kindler thinks, Sever can have a safe-conduct pass to leave the ghetto for his job each morning, and if an *Aktion* is imminent, he will be able to escape in time.

Shmelke writes us that he has made arrangements for Sever, even though some of his friends at the railroad objected. They know the boy is skinny and frail and they may have to cover up for him. The stationmaster also didn't want Sever. But luckily, Shmelke is on friendly terms with the SS officer in command of the station, a man by the name of Weisbauer. Perhaps Weisbauer has befriended Shmelke because he knows that the Polish workers at the station like him, so Shmelke could be useful some day. At any rate, Weisbauer often asks Shmelke to harness his horses to his sleigh and, if he doesn't happen to have one of his Gestapo friends with him, he gives Shmelke a ride into town at the end of the day. Sometimes Weisbauer even allows Shmelke to load bags of flour onto the sleigh, to smuggle into the ghetto on the way home. On the strength of this friendship, Shmelke brought Sever Kindler to Weisbauer and asked him whether the boy could have a job. When Weisbauer saw young Kindler, he laughed and looked at Shmelke as if he'd gone crazy. "They need workers at this station, not boys to post the train schedules," he said. But a gift of money given him by Shmelke from Dr. Kindler helped change his mind, and now Sever Kindler is working at the railroad station. Dr. Kindler is very grateful to Shmelke and they are now close friends.

All the doctors in the ghetto are living in one house, across the street from the place where the Letzters are now living.

● ● ●

We are freezing in Mrs. Halamajowa's hayloft. Mrs. Halamajowa keeps bringing us hot water bottles, hot bricks and steaming hot coffee for a little warmth.

Judging from the notes Shmelke has been sending us through Mrs. Halamajowa, the situation in the ghetto is desperate now. There is hardly a home where someone hasn't come down with typhoid fever. Shmelke writes me the names of friends who have already died of the disease.

Three men—two of them young, one a little older—have been appointed as a burial squad to remove the dead from the houses in the ghetto. The bodies are loaded onto a horse-drawn wagon and placed into boxes large enough to hold five corpses at a time. The three men spend all day collecting the dead. The Jewish cemetery is at the edge of the ghetto. On the way back from the cemetery, the burial squad has to pass through a street in the "Aryan" sector. There they buy groceries from Gentile stores and put them into the empty box that held the dead they have just buried. That's how a little food is smuggled into the ghetto from the world outside. When I lived in the ghetto, I sometimes gave the burial squad an order for groceries, but I couldn't afford to do it often because it was too expensive.

In the hayloft, February, 1943

During the night of Saturday, February 6, my brother Shmelke comes to us in the hayloft and stays until morning. He wants me to give him several gold rings and a gold watch of mine to sell because the family in the ghetto needs cash.

Shmelke also has other news to report. The local landowner sent a wagon-load of firewood to Issacher Spalter as a gift from an honest Gentile to a long-time Jewish friend. The Gestapo seized the firewood, arrested Spalter and then shot him.

On Sunday morning, Shmelke returns to his job at the railroad station.

• • •

On Wednesday, February 10, Mrs. Halamajowa brings us a note from Shmelke in which he writes that he probably won't be coming to see us for a few weeks because he has come down with a slight cold. We're afraid it's typhoid fever. In his weakened condition I don't see how he could survive that. Also, since he was with us at such close quarters in the hayloft only a few days ago, we wonder whether we will catch the disease. If we contract typhoid fever, it will be the end for us also.

• • •

Eight days have passed and we haven't gotten sick yet, but we are desperately worried because we have no news from my mother, Leah and Shmelke in the ghetto. I ask Mrs. Halamajowa to go to the barbed wire fence that encloses the ghetto and motion to someone inside to go get a member of our family so we can find out how Shmelke is. But nobody comes to her. We now suspect that not only Leah and Shmelke, but also my mother, is sick.

• • •

Three days later, Mrs. Halamajowa comes to us in the hayloft with a note from Shmelke which she says that Dr. Kindler gave her for us. Shmelke writes that he expects to be up and about in a few days. Our mother has kidney trouble and Leah is suffering from pains in her legs. Dr. Kindler has added a few lines informing me that Shmelke is not seriously ill and should be back at work in a couple of days.

The news from the family is a relief, but now there's something else to worry about. Since Dr. Kindler gave Shmelke's note to Mrs. Halamajowa, the doctor obviously knows where we are hiding. The thought that one more person knows about it has given me a couple of sleepless nights. Until now, not even our closest friends knew where we have gone, but now everybody will soon know.

• • •

On Saturday, February 27, Mrs. Halamajowa brings me a brief note from Shmelke informing me that he had gone back to work. He himself handed her the note. Mrs. Halamajowa says that Shmelke looks terrible and can hardly stand on his feet. My mother and Leah have added a few lines to prove to me that they are really still alive. This is more than just a sign of life. Shmelke writes that both Mother and Leah are still bedridden but "out of danger."

Shmelke's next note gives us additional details. All the 17 people living in our ghetto building came down with typhoid fever. There was no one to look after them. During the night, the patients became delirious. It was like a madhouse—wild screams everywhere. Shmelke says he was slightly out of his head himself with fever and, at one point, was clawing at his own body. Isaac, Itshi Letzter's brother, tied his hands with wire so he shouldn't injure himself. He was ready to tear the whole house down. It was freezing cold and there was no food. One neighbor took pity on the patients and brought potatoes into the building: one potato for each person. The people were virtually dying from thirst.

Altshe, Shlomo Schuman's wife, that wonderful woman, burst into tears when she came there and saw what was going on. Despite Dr. Kindler's stern warnings that anyone who set foot inside that typhoid-infested building had better prepare to meet his Maker, Altshe came every day with food for the patients.

According to Shmelke, Altshe thinks I'm crazy to have left the ghetto and split up my family. Once she said, "Moshe Maltz used to sell cattle. That's probably why he has no more brains than a calf."

One night, when his fever had reached 40° Centigrade [104° F.], Shmelke called Dr. Kindler to his bedside, took his hand and made him swear not to tell anybody that he, Shmelke, had told him where we were hiding, and not to abandon our mother and Leah in the ghetto. He also gave Dr. Kindler the rings and the gold watch I had given him before he got sick. Shmelke really thought he was dying, so he wanted Dr. Kindler to sell the gold and see that we received the cash.

• • •

More news from Shmelke: They've started killing Jews again in the ghetto. A group of Jews were taken to the Jewish cemetery, ordered to dig their own graves, and then shot. Among the dead is Meir Shafransky, deputy chairman of the *Judenrat*. Seemann, the same Gestapo gangster who shot my friends Efraim Windler and Moshe Weber, made Shafransky squat on the ground and then put a bullet in him.

March, 1943

Apparently the strategy of the Nazi murderers is to finish off the *Judenrat* and other Jewish privileged characters whom they used to leave unscathed. Shmelke writes that a high-ranking Gestapo officer by the name of Reiman came into the ghetto one night and demanded to see Bronstein, the chief of the Jewish police. Someone ran to get Bronstein. When Bronstein appeared, Reiman simply walked up to him and put a bullet in his head. Bronstein still ran a few yards before he fell dead.

The next day, Seemann caught Joseph Gross, a member of the Jewish police, looking the other way while Bronstein's widow passed through the ghetto gate. Seemann strode up to Gross and shot him.

The night before, some drunk Gestapo men entered the ghetto, broke into several houses and shot nine Jews. They missed one child, so they beat him to death with a heavy iron rod.

One night, Shmelke writes, a Gestapo man walked into *Judenrat* headquarters and asked, "Which one of you bought the whiskey we ordered?" Somebody pointed to a member of the Jewish police. It seems the Gestapo hadn't liked the whiskey, so the Gestapo officer shot the Jewish policeman on the spot.

• • •

A primitive hospital has been set up in the ghetto. The Jews in this hospital are dying of starvation. Shmelke writes that Mottel Gelbart is a patient there, too, and that he, Shmelke, visited him there. Shmelke took some candy—heaven knows where he got it—to the hospital and distributed it among the patients, who thanked him profusely and wished him a long life.

So Mottel Gelbart, once known as the wealthiest Jew in Sokal, is starving in a ghetto hospital. . . .

Altshe Schuman has died of typhoid fever. Shmelke brought her a lemon from one of the railroad men. She greedily tore into it with her fingers. She lasted twelve days and then she died. I think that's the way she wanted it. She said that nowadays it's a luxury to be able to die in your own bed.

In the hayloft, April, 1943

Spring is coming. The cold is gone, but now we have other problems. There are no windows in the hayloft, so we have hardly any air to breathe. What we do have is fleas that make their home in the hay and keep us awake all night long.

I look out through a crack in the wall and see the Gentiles tending their gardens. Their children are scampering around barefooted. It makes my heart ache. These children outside are playing in the sunshine and the fresh air, while my little Chaim is cooped up in that dark, stuffy hayloft.

In the distance I can see a column of humanity marching off to work under guard—my fellow Jews in Sokal. What a contrast—the Gentiles are free to enjoy this beautiful spring, while the Jews must do slave labor and figure out tricks to escape the fate the Nazi murderers are planning for them. We want survive, but who knows how much longer we can hold out?

The Gentiles working in the gardens outside are laughing and probably exchanging the latest news about Jews being killed in Lvov, Cracow and Warsaw. Sometimes Mrs. Halamajowa goes out and talks with these people. I strain my ears to listen to how they really feel about us Jews.

One Gentile is digging up a tree. He has joined the conversation. "Who needs this garbage?" he says. By "garbage," of course, he means the Jews. A chill goes through me. All this talk may have a bad influence on Mrs. Halamajowa.

That evening, when she brings us our supper, I watch her face closely for any change after those conversations in the garden. But I see no change in her expression or behavior.

The next day she brings us our breakfast and lunch again, as usual. Still no change in her face or manner. Finally I work up the courage to ask her who the character was that referred to the Jews as "garbage." She replies, "Don't mind him. He's a fool."

• • •

Our "neighbors," the three pigs in the pigsty below our hayloft, are getting too big and destructive. Mrs. Halamajowa thinks the time has come to slaughter them and replace them with three younger pigs.

One morning when she brings our breakfast, Mrs. Halamajowa announces that a slaughterer will come later in the day to kill the three pigs. He'll be working in the pigsty directly below us; therefore we must be especially quite and move as little as we can, so the slaughterer shouldn't hear us and ask questions.

After a while, we hear Mrs. Halamajowa entering the pigsty, talking with a man. Judging from their conversation, it is the slaughterer. Soon we hear the pigs squealing, but this slaughterer appears to be an expert at his job because the squeals soon stop. He and Mrs. Halamajowa work all day long skinning the carcasses and cutting up the meat. She will send some of the meat to her sisters, who don't have any money. We, too, will be living on that pork for the next several weeks.

I feel uneasy about Mrs. Halamajowa having the pigs slaughtered in her own home. To slaughter pigs in your own home is against the law and subject to the death penalty. But our Mrs. Halamajowa isn't afraid of anyone. She says the neighbors wouldn't dare report her because they think she is a *Volksdeutsche*, an ethnic German, which gives her a privileged status.

• • •

Mrs. Halamajowa has told us that she will leave town on April 20th to visit her son for the Easter holidays. Her daughter Hela will look after us while she is gone. I am worried, but there's nothing we can do to change the situation.

On April 20th, Mrs. Halamajowa bids us farewell and leaves as planned. Hela is working at the post office each day until noon, when she comes home. You can tell her mother is away. The food isn't so good because Hela has to do the cooking quickly and on the sly. She has a boyfriend who comes to visit her. He is a vicious anti-Semite; she is afraid he may become suspicious and ask her who needs all this food in the house. She also can't bring the food to us while he is around because he follows her wherever she goes.

• • •

On Easter Sunday, I hear someone talking in German outside. I freeze with fear. I strain my ears to listen. It's only Hela, talking in German with some man, and the conversation sounds casual and light-hearted. After a while they stop talking. That evening, when Hela brings supper, I ask her who the man was with whom I heard her talking. She explains it was her boss from the post office. He came to visit and she took a picture of him.

• • •

At the end of the month, Mrs. Halamajowa returns from her visit to her son. She brings startling news: the Jews in the Warsaw Ghetto have launched a revolt against the Germans. They won't allow the Germans to take them alive.

She has other news, too: the people she met as she passed through Lvov say that the war may still last a long, long time.

In the hayloft, May, 1943

Shmelke writes that things are worse again in the Sokal ghetto. The Gestapo has confiscated the safe-conduct passes that made it possible for some Jews to go to their jobs outside the ghetto on their own, without German or Ukrainian escorts. All Jews must now go to their places of work in groups escorted by German or Ukrainian guards. As a result, Shmelke can no longer stop at Mrs. Halamajowa's house with messages for us. So Mrs. Halamajowa will go to the railroad station to give him letters from us and bring back messages from him.

All the towns in the immediate environment of Sokal are already *judenrein.* Shmelke writes that the Jewish post office has been closed because there are not enough Jews left to use it.

• • •

Dr. Kindler has asked Shmelke again to find a hideout for him. Shmelke has told Mrs. Halamajowa about him. She says she would take the doctor into her hayloft but there would be no room for his wife and two sons.

• • •

Three young people were sent from the ghetto to the Wolyn woods to make contact with partisan resistance fighters. They discovered partisans who said they would allow Jews to join them in their camp. As a result, a group of 13 Jews left the ghetto and made for the woods. A few days later, two of them came back. The partisans had turned out to be followers of the Ukrainian Fascist leader, Bandera, a rabid anti-Semite. They murdered all the Jews from the group except those two, who managed to escape.

So much for any hopes the Jews in the ghetto may have pinned on the partisan fighters. The young people still left in the Sokal ghetto feel let down; they had planned to escape into the woods and join the partisans, but now that they knew who these partisans are, they have become desperate. Some youngsters have bought revolvers from Polish arms smugglers so they can shoot at least some of the Nazi and Ukrainian murderers before they themselves are killed.

There are Jews in the ghetto who wonder whether it is all worthwhile; perhaps they should end their lives right now. They can't stand the tortures of hunger. Death seems to them the only way out. But other Jews in the ghetto are building bunkers where they can hold out for months, if necessary. They feel sure that the next *Aktion* in Sokal will be the longest, because it will be the last.

• • •

Shmelke goes to work at the railroad every day with a group of other workers, under guard. He writes he's still looking for Gentiles who would give shelter to Dr. Kindler and his family, but no one seems willing to do that. Dr. Pellach, a Ukrainian doctor who shared Dr. Kindler's practice and claimed to be a friend, had one piece of advice to give him: get yourself some poison and put an end to it all.

There are four Kindlers: Dr. David Kindler; his wife, Clara; and their two sons, Sever (Simcha), who is fourteen and Eli, who is four. Eli has just been sent back to the Sokal ghetto from Zamosc, where he was hidden in a Polish convent.

I get all this news from Shmelke's notes which he passes to Mrs. Halamajowa at the railroad station. I have written to Shmelke (via Mrs. Halamajowa) that he and the rest of the family should now leave the ghetto and move in with us, into Mrs. Halamajowa's hayloft. But Shmelke won't listen to me. Dr. Kindler has been turning his head. Kindler wants to send his wife and two sons to safety, but he's changed his mind about going into hiding himself. He says he'll get advance warning—how, I don't know—when an *Aktion* is imminent, and he will then be able to escape before anything happens.

I know the reason for Kindler's change of heart. He feels he is such a prominent personality that the Jews in the ghetto watch his every move as an indication of things to come, and then they act accordingly. If he runs away, they will think an *Aktion* is imminent. He is afraid that if rumors of an *Aktion* then turn out to be false, the people will be so furious with him for having driven them into hysteria that he would never be able to show his face in the ghetto again.

• • •

I keep writing to Shmelke to leave the ghetto with Mother, Leah and Feyge Chashe, but he still won't listen.

At last, on May 24, Mrs. Halamajowa returns from the railroad station with a letter from Shmelke informing us that the people of Sokal are expecting an *Aktion* any day now. There have been *Aktionen* in Bisk and Brody on the previous Thursday and Friday, and those two cities are in the same Gestapo district as Sokal. This time, Shmelke finally understands, the *Aktion* in Sokal won't stop until there are no more Jews left there. In Bisk and Brody the Germans have already murdered all the Jews, including the members and workers of the *Judenrat* and the Jewish police.

In Sokal all the Jews with "essential" jobs have been moved into a house that was once the home of Moshe Pass, which is outside the ghetto area. That's where they now eat and sleep; they are not permitted to return to their homes in the ghetto after work. This, too, is a sign that the end of the ghetto is near. The Germans need these skilled Jewish workers and don't want them killed or deported when the ghetto is liquidated. The members of the *Judenrat* in Sokal are in despair; they are sure that this is the end of our Jewish community.

As I read Shmelke's letter, I know there is only one thing for Shmelke and me to do: we must save all members of our family before it is too late.

• • •

On May 25th, Mrs. Halamajowa comes up to us and reports that Shmelke has just been at her place. He has asked her to leave the key to the hayloft in the backyard near the outhouse because the family will be coming to the hayloft tonight. Shmelke took his life in his hands when he left his work at the railroad station without permission to bring his message to Mrs. Halamajowa, but he felt he had nothing to lose.

That night, the ghetto was in a state of feverish activity once again, with people hurrying through the streets, moving their possessions into the bunkers they had prepared as places of refuge.

Shmelke went to see Dr. Kindler and urged him to escape with our family.

Dr. Kindler suggested that Shmelke move into the bunker with him and help him equip the bunker in the ghetto where Kindler explained he would take shelter in case of an *Aktion*. He and his family would spend the daytime hours at their home in the ghetto and move into the bunker only for the night, when the Germans would search the ghetto dwellings and drag the Jews from their beds. Kindler was still apprehensive about what would happen to him if there was no *Aktion*. He did not want to make a fool of himself before the Jewish community by turning chicken, as he saw it. Shmelke helped Kindler carry several packages of groceries, which kindler had stored in his home earlier, into the bunker.

In Shmelke's opinion, Kindler's bunker was probably the best shelter inside the ghetto. Located in the cellar of Yossel Gontis, on Konotop Street, it could hold 50 persons. As Shmelke entered the bunker with Kindler's packages, someone shouted, "So, Shmelke Maltz, you want to move in with us, too? We have news for you: you can't. As far as we're concerned, the doctor can go to hell also."

When Shmelke came in, Kindler's bunker was already crowded. Each person sat on whatever baggage he had brought. There was not a breath of fresh air. Some women felt faint; others were crying for water. After a few minutes' deliberation, Shmelke asked himself, "Do I really want to move into this hellhole?" He promptly turned and went back outside.

"I don't care what you and your family do, doctor, but I won't move into this bunker with you. I'm getting out of here fast," Shmelke said to Kindler. "I want to leave the ghetto. I don't want to be trapped in the ghetto and be killed with my mother, my sister and the rest of the family." Kindler then had another change of heart. He hugged and kissed Shmelke and said, "Well, I won't move into this bunker either. I'll go with you wherever you will go." Kindler left all his groceries in the bunker and took with him only his medical bag and a few personal belongings.

And so Kindler, his wife and two sons, my mother, my sister Leah and her little Feyge Chashe, and Shmelke, set out for Mrs. Halamajowa's hayloft. Shmelke left some of his own meager belongings behind; he couldn't carry them all, because he had to carry Eli, Dr. Kindler's little son.

When Shmelke left the bunker, he met Susia Kellan, a lawyer's daughter. She asked Shmelke whether he had a place to go. When she heard that Shmelke had been driven out of the bunker, she suggested that he come with her to her own hiding place.

As the group headed for the bank of the River Bug, Shmelke said to Dr. Kindler, "I have a police saber. I hope you have some knives in your medical bag. Better take them out and let us hold them in readiness. We may have to use them if someone stops us on the way."

• • •

That night I lay in the hayloft and cannot sleep. At about one o'clock in the morning I hear the crunch of footsteps on the gravel from Mrs. Halamajowa's backyard. Then I hear the door of the pigsty open. My family has arrived! This must mean that the Jews of Sokal know the end has come.

The door of our hayloft is unlocked from the outside. I open the door and see eight people at the foot of the ladder leading up to our hayloft: my mother, Shmelke, Leah, Feyge Chashe and the four Kindlers. I first help Dr. Kindler up the ladder, then all the others and finally, I help carry their packages into the hayloft.

I am really frightened that someone might be spying on us. There are now 13 of us in Mrs. Halamajowa's hayloft, in a space of one middle-sized room with a six-foot-high ceiling, four Kindlers, my whole family and myself. We lie wide awake the rest of the night, listening for sounds from the ghetto, which is only one kilometer away. Has the *Aktion* already begun?

• • •

In the morning, Mrs. Halamajowa comes up with breakfast for all of us. The door of the hayloft is unlocked, so she knows that all her "guests" have arrived. Her garden has just been newly planted, so she goes down into the backyard with a rake and smooths the ground to erase the footprints of the new arrivals.

By now it is clear that the dreaded *Aktion* had not materialized in the ghetto. So the panic of the night before was unwarranted. I look through a crack in the wall of the hayloft. I see a column of people marching under guard from the ghetto to their work on the railroad as usual, and another column, also under guard, moving in the direction of the Podhoretz woods. So, life in the Sokal ghetto seems to be running its normal course.

Mrs. Halamajowa brings us lunch. The four Kindlers don't eat a bite. They seem deep in thought, watching us, observing how we live in the hayloft. They had a relatively good life in the ghetto, with a comfortable home and fairly decent food. I wonder whether they could adjust to life in this hayloft.

Dr. Kindler removes various boxes and vials from his medical bag and studies their contents. Has he left out anything important? There is a lot of aspirin for all kinds of pain and fever; cough syrup; injections for the heart; pills for stomach trouble and pills to put restless children to sleep. He has also brought vials of poison for all of us to take if the Germans discover our hideout. We don't want the murderers to have the satisfaction of capturing us alive.

Meanwhile, Mrs. Halamajowa is bustling about her pigsty and her house, looking as busy and excited as the mother of a bride after all her wedding guests have arrived. She is looking for large pots and kettles in which to cook for 13 people. She also brings up additional buckets for our toilet needs. Then she runs out to shop for groceries.

• • •

In the afternoon, Dr. Kindler and wife talk to each other in low whispers. In the evening, Kindler says to Shmelke, "Shmelke, you'll have to take me and my family back to the ghetto tonight. I don't think we can stand this." Shmelke replies, "All right. I'll take you back later." When Mrs. Halamajowa brings us our supper we ask her not to lock the hayloft from the outside for the night because the Kindlers have decided to return to the ghetto after dark.

In the evening, as the Kindlers prepare to leave, I have a brainstorm. I'll suggest to Dr. Kindler that he and his family should give the hayloft a chance and stay for at least another day. I want to stall for time because I am afraid that if Shmelke accompanies the Kindlers back to the ghetto, he may be trapped there. So I move up close to Kindler and whisper to him, "Listen to me, doctor. Stay with us for one more day. Maybe you'll get used to it." Kindler thinks for a while, then says, "All right, we'll stay. Let's all go to sleep now."

Just before midnight I hear a rumble of trucks from the highway. "Do you hear those trucks outside?" I ask Kindler. "The murderers from Lvov are heading for our ghetto." We can't go back to sleep anymore.

• • •

At two o'clock, Thursday morning, May 27, we hear a series of explosions. It sounds to me as if the Germans are lobbing hand grenades into cellars where they think Jews may be hiding. We lie motionless, as if turned to stone. Before long, we hear shouts and screams from the direction of the ghetto.

Later, Mrs. Halamajowa brings us our breakfast and says, "The *Aktion* is on." We ask Mrs. Halamajowa not to bring us any more food today because we don't feel like eating.

We hear shooting all day long. We feel as if every shot has gone through our own hearts. We know that each bullet will hit one of our own people in the ghetto. We hear screams—Jews screaming, struggling against death. Mixed with these sounds of pain and horror we hear singing and music. Ukrainian schoolchildren are parading through the streets. They seem to be celebrating something—is it the death of the Jews in the ghetto?

At noon Mrs. Halamajowa's daughter Hela comes home from her job at the post office. She reports that all the other clerks have gone to the ghetto to watch the show and see the dead Jews. They asked Hela to come, too, but she couldn't find it in her heart to go with them.

The *Aktion* continues all day long. Later, we get the details: Anyone who attempted to offer resistance was shot. Yehiel Zinz preferred death to the humiliation of being ordered to strip naked at gunpoint. So he hit one of the Gestapo man and they hacked him to pieces with an axe.

My old school friend Dr. Babad was caught hiding out in an attic; the Germans tossed him out the window and then shot him. The Jews were herded onto trucks and driven out to the Tartakow highway, three kilometers from Sokal. The trucks stopped in front of a deep, wide ditch, apparently left from the trench warfare with the Soviets. On one side of the ditch stood a large chest into which the Jews were ordered to place all their money and valuables. After that, everyone was ordered to strip naked. Sitting to one side of the ditch was a German operating a machine gun, with a cigarette dangling from his mouth, obviously bored and doing his job as a matter of mechanical routine. He shot ten Jews at a time. The next ten had to dump the bodies of the dead onto a pile of corpses like so many bales of hay before they themselves were shot. So that was the destination of the trucks we heard rumbling over the highway all day long.

Several hundred Jews were marched to the cemetery on Switeszower Street. Some tried to escape, but were gunned down. At the end of the day the Schupo men from Lvov were replaced by German and Ukrainian police who guarded the ghetto all day and all night while Jews were being rounded up. The Jews were herded into the prison. Each day an additional truckload of Jews was driven from the prison to an execution site outside the town and shot.

The murderers used the services of a Jewish informer, a boy of fifteen. He was crawling among the ghetto ruins, looking for Jews. If he found Jews, he asked them for money and then he reported them to the Gestapo. The Jews in the bunkers knew all about him and slammed the door into his face whenever he appeared for a handout. The last time this happened, the door was slammed into his face so hard that his neck was broken and he died.

Gentiles were assigned to burial squads to bury the Jews who had been ordered to dig their own graves before being shot. I was told that the soil was heaving for hours after such mass burials; some of the victims had been buried alive and survived for a while before the soil and other bodies finally smothered them.

Dr. Falik, that fine, pious man who used to bring food to the boys in the labor camp, went crazy in the bunker where Dr. Kindler would have hidden out if we let him return to the ghetto. Falik ran around screaming, "Give me my diploma, somebody! Give me my diploma!"

The Jewish police was transferred from the ghetto to a camp outside. They knew this meant they would be murdered the next day, after the Jews inside the ghetto had been finished off. So, during the night, they escaped and headed for the woods.

Special skills were no longer a guarantee of survival. Jewish artisans and craftsmen were shot, as were several hundred Jews who had escaped form the Sokal ghetto to Wolin, in the Pritzk district. The Ukrainians murdered them all.

Posters appeared all over Sokal announcing that the town was now *judenrein* and that anyone giving food or shelter to Jewish "fugitives" was subject to the death penalty. Any Aryan who knew of Jews hidden at the home of a neighbor had to report the fact to the nearest police station.

On Friday, May 28th, the day after the *Aktion*, we are still numb with shock and horror. There are still sporadic bursts of gunfire from the ghetto. Mrs. Halamajowa and her daughter Hela are running back and forth between the house and the pigsty, listening for sounds from our hayloft to make sure we are quiet so the neighbors shouldn't hear us.

My little four-year-old niece, Leah's daughter Feyge Chashe, won't stop crying. We all beg her to keep quiet. We give her toys (Hela's holiday gifts) to divert her, but nothing helps.

Mrs. Halamajowa comes up to us and says, "For mercy's sake, can't you people make that child stop crying? Do you want the Germans to find you and kill us all?" She takes a stick and begins to beat the piglets she has brought in place of the ones she slaughtered. She hopes their squeaks of pain will drown out the sound of Feyge Chashe's crying.

The hours go by Feyge Chashe is still crying. We are all terrified. Mrs. Halamajowa and Hela are still beating the piglets but how much longer can they keep this up? And how much longer will the poor little pigs be able to stand this?

At about eight o'clock that evening Mrs. Halamajowa knocks on our hayloft door with her stick. We open the door. "You'll have to do something," she says, very much upset. "If this crying goes on, it'll be the end for all of us." We promise her that we will "do something." After she has left, we huddle together and discuss what we should do.

We come to a terrible decision. We will have to kill Feyge Chashe with poison from Dr Kindler's medical bag. We can't endanger 14 other lives—those of our family, the Kindlers and the two Halamajowa's—because of one child. We report our decision to Mrs. Halamajowa. She doesn't say a word. What could she say? Feyge Chashe goes on crying.

We cover Feyge Chashe with blankets. Dr. Kindler pours a spoonful of poison from one of his vials and forces the spoon between Feyge Chashe's lips. Feyge Chashe makes a face, spits it out—and keeps on crying.

Finally, some of the poison seems to stay in. After a few minutes, Feyge Chashe stops crying. Her eyes fall shut. She appears unconscious. She does not seem to be breathing. We all squat around the little figure lying on the straw as if we were already sitting *shiva** after

---

* Lit., "seven." The seven days of mourning observed by the immediate family following a funeral. During that period of intense mourning, observant Jews do not use chairs but sit on low stools or on boxes, or squat on the floor.

the funeral. No one makes a sound. My sister Leah, Feyge Chashe's mother, does not weep. "I forgive you for what you have done to my child," she whispers, "as long as God forgives you, too." One life for a chance to save 14 other lives. . . .

Two hours later—at about ten o'clock—Mrs. Halamajowa comes to us holding out a large burlap bag. "The child's soul is with God now," she says in a voice that betrays no emotion. "Put her in this bag. I'll bury her."

Dr. Kindler leans forward to pick up the limp little body from the straw. As he touches the child, his sensitive hands feel something unexpected. He motions to me and whispers in my ear, "There's a pulse! It's faint, but I can feel it! This child is alive!"

It takes a moment to grasp what the doctor is saying. Then I say that if the child wasn't killed by the dose of poison he gave her, it is nothing short of a miracle. Feyge Chashe was meant to live.

When we tell Mrs. Halamajowa that Feyge Chashe is not dead but merely unconscious, she agrees that it must be God's will that this child should survive. "I hope she doesn't start crying again when she comes to," she says. "I can assure you I won't allow her to cry again," says my sister Leah. These are the first words Leah has spoken in almost two hours. Then she clasps her child in her arms and bursts into sobs.

At about three in the morning, Feyge Chashe regains consciousness and starts crying again. "Mama, I'm alive," she says. Leah rocks her in her arms and tries to comfort her. "Give me some blankets," she finally whispers to no one in particular. I hand her as many of our blankets as I can hold at a time. Leah piles them on Feyge Chashe. We no longer hear her crying.

The next morning Feyge Chashe is wide awake, very pale, but otherwise apparently unharmed except for some blisters on her lips. "Superficial burns," says Dr. Kindler. "From the poison." She probably did not swallow enough of the poison to kill her. She must have spat nearly all of it out. But who could have seen that in the pitch darkness of the hayloft?

We now have a plan to follow if Feyge Chashe should start to cry again. We will cover her head with as many blankets as possible—not tightly enough to smother her, but enough to muffle the sound. If that doesn't help, we will give her a cup of water with sleeping powder from Dr. Kindler's bag. But only a very, very little sleeping powder because God seems to have intended that Feyge Chashe should live.

• • •

Dr. Kindler is trying to improve sanitary conditions in our hayloft. He has pried loose two shingles from the roof to let in a little fresh air and more daylight, which is important, especially for the children. He has asked Mrs. Halamajowa for two pieces of glass with which to close the empty spaces in the roof in case of rain.

Dr. Kindler insists that we frequently launder and change our underwear to prevent illnesses, especially typhoid fever which, he explains, thrives wherever hygiene is poor. Mrs. Halamajowa brings us extra buckets for doing our laundry and taking "baths," if you can call it that. My wife has been sewing pants for Shmelke, Chaim and me from burlap bags donated by Mrs. Halamajowa. Chana also gives us men haircuts whenever she thinks we need it.

The fleas are multiplying at an appalling rate. They are small but very hardy creatures; you can't kill them by stepping on them or crushing them between your fingers. We have found another way. Each one of us has a little cup of water. When we wake up in the morning, we pick the fleas from our blankets, clothes and bodies and dunk them in the water until they drown. But it doesn't do much good. These creatures insist on keeping us awake at night and feeding on our flesh.

In the hayloft, June, 1943

The slightest sound from us could betray our presence to Mrs. Halamajowa's neighbors. A sneeze, a cough or even a gentle snore from one person could give us all away. Dr. Kindler had taught us the trick of closing our nostrils with our fingers to stifle a sneeze, and he dispenses cough syrup from his bag for the very first cough he hears from anyone. Each night one of us stays up to awaken snorers. The three mothers—my wife, my sister Leah and Mrs. Kindler—keep their little ones close behind them to make sure they won't cry.

• • •

Mrs. Halamajowa has trouble getting food for us because of the wartime rationing. There is also a severe shortage of firewood. Mrs. Halamajowa's son comes every four weeks with kerosene, machine oil, olive oil and cottonseed oil for his mother to give the peasants in exchange for food. He also brings his mother dried firewood. German workers from the oil refinery where he is manager make the trip with him; they help him transport the wood and pile it up in his mother's backyard. Little do these Germans know that the firewood will be used to cook food for Jews!

We are uneasy about Mrs. Halamajowa's barter deals because it is against the law, and if she gets caught, it'll be the end not only for her but for all of us. But she insists that her neighbors wouldn't dare report her to the authorities because they think she is a fervent Nazi.

Each morning she still takes her rake and mixes the waste from our buckets with the slop from her pigs and chickens so that no one should suspect the presence of 13 human beings in her hayloft.

• • •

Dr. Kindler still isn't happy here. He doesn't like our living conditions and sometimes I think he also doesn't find the company of us ordinary people too congenial. He would leave the hayloft with his family if he could find another place to hide.

One day he says to me, "I don't know what I should do. I have very little cash with me here. I have more money, of course, but I've left it with Gentile friends for safekeeping." Does he think, perhaps, that if he could get his hands on that money, he could give it all to one Gentile in return for shelter at a fancier place than Mrs. Halamajowa's hayloft? He says he doesn't know whom to trust. He has heard stories of Gentiles giving shelter to Jews after having taken all their money, and either murdering their "guests" themselves or handing them over to the Germans.

Because he doesn't really trust anyone, Dr. Kindler has distributed most of his money among three different individuals for safekeeping. He says that once he settled down with people he considers worthy of his trust, he will have all the money sent to him bit by bit. At present, one part of his money is in Warsaw, with a Mr. Decker, who once was a court clerk in Sokal. Another part is with a nurse who is now living in a convent in Lvov, but once worked at the hospital in Sokal. The third part is with another nurse, who is now working at the Sokal hospital.

Dr. Kindler wants to send Mrs. Halamajowa to retrieve some of his money, but I explain to him that we had better lie low for the time being because the Germans and the Ukrainians are surely still on the lookout for Jews in the Sokal area.

We can't make contact with the world outside because more and more Jews are being arrested and killed every day. I have explained to Dr. Kindler that we still have some cash left and Mrs. Halamajowa still has some of our belongings to sell for food. So we have enough to live on for a while. For the present, it isn't necessary for him to send for any of his reserves.

In the hayloft, July, 1943

In addition to cooking for the 13 of us, Mrs. Halamajowa brings us ripe vegetables from her garden. She also buys us berries from out-of-town Gentiles who happen to pass through Sokal.

Once every few days, when she has finished her housework, Mrs. Halamajowa comes to us in the hayloft just to talk. She tells us the latest news, for instance, that Jews from this village or that have been rounded up and brought to Gestapo headquarters in Sokal. She says that posters have appeared all over Sokal announcing that anyone who hands a Jew over to the police will receive a reward: five liters of whiskey, along with some cash. That's the kind of news Mrs. Halamajowa has for us these days.

Every afternoon she brings us the daily newspapers. What interests us most are the official communiqués from the *Wehrmacht*, the latest news from the Eastern front and Africa, and Allied air raids on Germany.

One day the newspapers carry a report that the Germans are "adjusting" and "shortening" their battle lines on the Eastern front. This must mean that the Germans have been forced to make a major retreat from the Russians. So the Germans are running away. We are happy.

Mrs. Halamajowa has brought us a map of the Eastern front. I study the map and figure out how far the battle lines are from us now. We see that the Russians are still about 1,500 kilometers away. Therefore, even assuming that, with luck, the Russians will advance steadily from now at a rate of 30 kilometers each day, it'll be another five months or so before they get to Sokal. It'll be hard for us to hold out that long. Every day seems like a year.

• • •

My youngest sister, Chaye Dvora, has been sick since June 22. The first few weeks we thought she was just in a run-down condition, but now it is clear that she is seriously ill.

Life in the hayloft has become extremely difficult. At first we were afraid to tell Mrs. Halamajowa that Chaye Dvora was sick because we didn't want to risk having her put us all out, but now we have had to tell her because we need not only medicines, but also better food for our patient.

The fleas and other parasites are multiplying. Meanwhile, Chaye Dvora is running a fever and has to stifle her coughs and groans. We take turns sitting up with her all night to make sure nobody hears her. Every couple of days Dr. Kindler gives her some medicines from the supplies he has brought with him, but what good does that do? We can't give Chaye Dvora what she really needs: fresh air and freedom.

Mother picks the fleas from Chaye Dvora's body each day. The fleas are literally sucking her blood and she is too weak to pick them off herself. Each evening Mrs. Halamajowa opens the door to the hayloft. We remove several shingles from the roof and we drag Chaye Dvora to a place where she can get that precious breath of fresh outdoor air even if it does smell from Mrs. Halamajowa's pigs.

Sundays and church holidays are the worst times for us because that's when the daughters of Mrs. Halamajowa's neighbors come with their boyfriends from Lvov to visit their parents. The girls are very close to the pigsty; we can hear them walking around, singing, laughing and making love with their boyfriends. In the meantime, we have to sit indoors, in the heat, watching each other so that no one outside should hear us breathe.

In the hayloft, August, 1943.

We are getting short of cash, and Mrs. Halamajowa needs the money for our food. Dr. Kindler has written a letter to the nurse at the convent in Lvov, asking for part of the money she has been keeping for him. Mrs. Halamajowa's daughter Hela makes the trip to Lvov to give the letter to the nurse. On her way home to Sokal, Hela stops at a pharmacy to buy medicine for Chaye Dvora. Dr. Kindler had written out a prescription for Hela to give to the pharmacist but he did not sign it. Two days later, Hela returns with the medicine from the pharmacy and the cash from the nurse in the convent.

This is the first time Hela will visit our hayloft since it has become so crowded. When her mother was away, she merely passed our food to us quickly through the door so her visiting boyfriend shouldn't notice. We had to make a little order so it shouldn't look too bad, and we cleaned up Chaye Dvora. But, when Hela comes in, she clasps her hand to her head. "How can people live like this?" she cries.

She gives the money and the medicine to Dr. Kindler. She has also bought some toys and candy for Chaim, Feyge Chashe and Eli. She sits down on the hay and we all gather around her to hear the latest news from Lvov.

Hela says that the Russian partisans are coming closer and are really hurting the Germans. Also, the Russians are shelling Warsaw. Nevertheless, the war will still last for a long time. Jews are still being arrested in Lvov. A family of Gentiles has been reported to the Gestapo for giving shelter to Jews. The entire family was arrested and had to march through the streets with posters hanging from their necks reading, "We are traitors. We gave shelter to Jews, the enemy of mankind." They were dragged through the streets of Lvov and then hanged.

• • •

Chaye Dvora is still sick. I think she has more fever now. We try to cheer her up. We tell her that everything will be all right soon because the reports from the Russian front are encouraging. A revolution has broken out in Italy against Mussolini and Allied troops are advancing in North Africa.

Most of the medicines Dr. Kindler has prescribed for Chaye Dvora are opiates so she should have no pain and be able to get some sleep. Dr. Kindler gives her a dose every few days. But now she is beginning to refuse the medicines. She seems to realize that Dr. Kindler can't help her. She only wants to know how much longer she will have to go on suffering and make us suffer with her.

Mrs. Halamajowa inquires each day how our patient is feeling. We keep telling her that my sister is improving so she shouldn't change her mind about letting all of us stay in the hayloft.

In the hayloft, Rosh HaShanah eve, September 29, 1943

On Monday, September 27, three days before Rosh HaShanah, our Jewish New Year, Dr. Kindler signals me to move closer to him; he has something to tell me. He thinks Chaye Dvora is dying. Later, at midnight, I hear Chaye Dvora whispering to our mother, who is lying close behind her in the straw, "Mama, I'm so hot!" My mother removes some of her blankets. But a few minutes later Chaye Dvora moans, "Mama, I'm so cold!" and Mother covers her again. Chaye Dvora is moaning nonstop now. Then, suddenly, silence in the hayloft. No more moaning, no more crying. I have just seen my youngest sister die.

What are we to do with the body? One of the Kindlers suggests that it should be lowered into the River Bug, which is virtually at Mrs. Halamajowa's doorstep. This could be done very quickly, late at night, when the town is asleep.

But how should we break the news to Mrs. Halamajowa? We've been lying to her all this time, telling her that Chaye Dvora was improving. And now. . . .

The next morning, Tuesday, September 28, when Mrs. Halamajowa brings us breakfast, we tell her about Chaye Dvora. She is upset, but she quickly regains her composure. She asks us not to tell her daughter Hela. She also feels that Chaye Dvora should have her final resting place in the ground and not simply be tossed into the river, as she puts it. My mother has nothing to say. She is still numb from the shock. Hitler has already taken her husband, her parents and her little granddaughter, Lifshe. Now her youngest daughter, too, is gone, dead at the age of 31.

Later in the day, we all take turns looking out through a crack in the wall of the hayloft. We watch Mrs. Halamajowa in her garden, under an apple tree, measuring out space for Chaye Dvora's grave.

At eight o'clock that night, when it is already pitch dark, Mrs. Halamajowa calls my brother Shmelke to come down into the garden and help her dig our sister's grave. Shmelke goes but Mrs. Halamajowa has to do the work by herself because Shmelke can't seem to make his hands work. When the grave is ready, he comes back to the hayloft. Together, he and I wrap our sister into the sheet on which she has lain all through her illness, and we carry her down into the garden. There, Shmelke, Mrs. Halamajowa and I bury Chaye Dvora under the apple tree. We quickly close the grave; no one must see us. After the grave is closed, Mrs. Halamajowa smooths the soil with her spade and her hands so that no one should notice anything out of the ordinary.

As we return to the pigsty, Mrs. Halamajowa begs us once again not to tell Hela because Hela would be afraid to go into the garden if she knew a body was buried there.

In the hayloft, October, 1943

Our mother never looks out through the crack in the hayloft wall anymore because she can't bear to see the apple tree beneath which her youngest daughter is buried.

. . .

From the day Sokal became *judenrein,* I have been keeping a Jewish religious calendar so I should not forget the dates of the Jewish holidays. I also note the date each Jewish month begins,* and the Sabbath immediately preceding each New Moon, when prayers for a healthy, happy month are recited at the synagogue.

With Chaye Dvora gone, we are only 12 in the hayloft now: eight adults (my mother, my sisters Yitte and Leah, my brother Shmelke, Chana, Dr. and Mrs. Kindler and myself), one teenager (Sever Kindler) and three young children (Eli Kindler, Feyge Chashe and Chaim). We have between us one single festival prayer book from which to recite the High Holiday prayers. We ask Mrs. Halamajowa not to bring us any food on Yom Kippur, the Day of Atonement, because we will be fasting on that day.

. . .

Fall has arrived, the fifth autumn of the war. Looking out through the crack in the hayloft wall, I can see Mrs. Halamajowa's neighbors outside, picking their ripe vegetables, while I am still in the hayloft with my family, looking out at the world through a crack in a wall. I saw them planting their winter crops last year and watched their vegetables grow. Now it's harvest time again and we are still in the dark, flea-infested hayloft with the end nowhere in sight.

Mrs. Halamajowa still brings us our meals each day. Potatoes are now the mainstay of our diet. We have potatoes three times daily.

It is clear to us that the war will continue through the winter and probably even through next summer. Mrs. Halamajowa is preparing for the winter. She has stored up flour and firewood. She has also bought wagonloads of newly-mowed hay. She has removed the old straw with the fleas from our hayloft and replaced it with the fresh hay. But somehow, the fleas are still with us.

Mrs. Halamajowa has also brought up bales of hay to place against the walls for insulation against winter drafts. We use some of this hay to plug up the little holes in the hayloft wall to keep out the winter winds and the snow during the coming winter months.

As I have said, it is certain that the war will continue at least through the winter, yet the Russian advance will continue, slowly but

---

* The Jewish calendar is based on the lunar year of 354 days. The months have 29 or 30 days each.

surely, because the Red Army has plenty of experience with winter warfare.

In the hayloft, November, 1943

Mrs. Halamajowa still brings us the daily newspapers every day. It is clear from the *Wehrmacht* communiqués that the Russians are advancing slowly but steadily.

• • •

It is getting cold, and Dr. Kindler and his family do not have winter blankets or warm clothes. Mrs. Halamajowa is willing to buy these things for them, but she can't do it without cash. So Dr. Kindler gives her a letter for the nurse at the hospital in Sokal who has part of his money. Mrs. Halamajowa does not tell the nurse that the Kindlers are in her hayloft; she says the letter was given to her by a woman in Lvov on behalf of Dr. Kindler.

The nurse has given the money to Mrs. Halamajowa, along with some underwear for the Kindlers, and a letter to the Kindlers in which she writes that the bad times will soon be over and that the Kindler family is always in her prayers.

Mrs. Halamajowa has bought blankets and warm boots for the Kindlers and brings them up to the hayloft. But she also has alarming news for us. Ukrainian nationalist groups in Wolyn, just a few kilometers from Sokal, have organized gangs; they call themselves "Banderowitzes" or "Bandera men" in honor of their leader, Stefan Bandera. They hate the Germans, but they also hate the Russians and the Jews. They are not discriminating about whom they kill; they are gunning down the populations of entire villages. The Germans aren't doing anything to stop the Bandera men. They are happy to have the nationality groups under their rule turn against each other and kill each other off.

Since there are hardly any Jews left to kill, the Bandera gangs have turned on the Poles. They are literally hacking the Poles to pieces. Each day, Mrs. Halamajowa says, you can see the bodies of Poles, with wires around their necks, floating down the River Bug.

Sokal is swamped with Poles who have run away from the Bandera gangs in Wolyn. The Poles who live in Sokal are taking these refugees into their homes, but they are afraid that the Bandera men will come to Sokal also and kill them, too.

This news frightens us because Mrs. Halamajowa is a Pole. If the

Bandera gangs come to Sokal, they might drive her out of her home, and what will become of us then?

• • •

It is bitter cold in the hayloft. We hope the bales of hay we've put up to insulate our walls will withstand the strong winter winds.

• • •

In the hayloft, December, 1943

Mrs. Halamajowa has brought us heated bricks and strong whiskey to keep us warm. I have been put in charge of the whiskey. It will be saved for special occasions. Whenever there's good news in the daily papers, we drink L'Chaim and wish each other that we may live to be liberated. We drink one such L'Chaim when we hear that the Germans have withdrawn from Kiev, the Ukrainian capital.

On December 6, St. Nicholas' Day, Mrs. Halamajowa gives toys and candy to Chaim, Feyge Chashe and the Kindler boys. The four children want to know how long it will be until the next Christian holiday; they like the candy.

Our neighbor, Benerowicz, is getting ready for the Christmas holiday. He got himself a couple of geese to fatten for his Christmas dinner, and he keeps them in the attic chamber that is separated from our hayloft by just a wooden plank. He comes up several times each day to feed his geese. This is very unpleasant. We always have to listen for his footsteps so we should be even quieter than usual when he comes.

Mrs. Halamajowa's pigs are ready for slaughter. This is the second pig-slaughtering session she has had since we've been here. But unlike last time, the three new piglets that are to replace the old pigs are already on hand. Mrs. Halamajowa is preparing the pork for the holidays. Unlike last time, she isn't selling any of the meat or giving it away. She will keep it all for us.

• • •

Mrs. Halamajowa's son and his wife have come for Christmas, along with several Germans who are working for him at the refinery. They have brought with them a barrel of kerosene and a barrel of oil for their mother to give to the peasants in exchange for the food we need. Mrs. Halamajowa has baked white rolls and sweet cakes for us. At midnight on Christmas Eve she comes to us carrying a bag filled with pastries. Then she goes back to her house and returns with a second bag of holiday goodies. The children love the pastries.

Mrs. Halamajowa also gives us a jar of rendered goose fat to spread on our bread.

Her son comes up to see us. He tells us about 40 Jews who were hiding out in the woods near his home. He says he gave them enough food to last them for at least half a year. But then the Bandera gangs came and murdered them all. After about half an hour, young Halamajowa wishes us good health and leaves us to our thoughts.

In the hayloft, January, 1944

The newspaper reports are vague. There are hints that the German battle lines are "flexible" or "movable." We understand this means that the Germans are retreating, but we don't know far the Russians have advanced. According to the reports, there is heavy fighting "in the southwest," but we can't make out exactly where.

Finally, one day early in January, we read a report, in print so small you hardly notice it, that the Germans have abandoned the town of Sarny. Sarny is only 240 kilometers east of Sokal. We are excited and elated. Maybe we'll live to see the end of this war after all.

Dr. Kindler says, "Moshe, bring out the whiskey." We drink *L'-Chaim* and cry from sheer joy. It seems that only a short time ago the Russians were still 2,000 kilometers away from us; now it's a mere 240. We tell Mrs. Halamajowa that the war can't last much longer now; we will soon be free. She is happy, too, because this means she is that much closer to receiving the reward I promised her a year ago for sheltering us: if I survive, I'll buy the other half of the house in which she lives and give it to her as a gift so she'll be the sole owner of her home.

But she also has disquieting news for us. She says that some Bandera gangs have already turned up in our area. She tells us how many Poles have already been killed by Bandera men in neighboring villages. In Konotop, for instance, the Banderists killed five Poles. At the funeral, while the local Polish priest was delivering the eulogy, a Bandera man, disguised in a German uniform, shot the priest right there at the graveside. The Bandera gangs don't want so much as one Pole left alive in our region.

• • •

There are rumors that Russian partisans have already been seen near Sokal. They don't kill civilians, only Germans. Already there are

Germans in the Sokal hospital who supposedly were wounded by Soviet partisans.

• • •

Mrs. Halamajowa is worried about herself, and about us. There is talk that the Bandera gangs are getting ready to attack Sokal and kill all its Polish inhabitants. If anything happens to Mrs. Halamajowa, what will become of us 12 unfortunates in her hayloft?

In the hayloft, February, 1944

One night we hear machine gun fire from various parts of Sokal. The shooting continues for about two hours.

The next morning we hear that Bandera gangs broke into the Gestapo headquarters and other German offices in Sokal. They tried to liberate several Ukrainians whom the Germans had arrested and placed into the town jail, but the Germans offered fierce resistance and the Bandera men had to withdraw.

Mrs. Halamajowa tells us that Poles from neighboring villages are still streaming into Sokal and the Poles living in Sokal are taking the refugees into their homes, but she, Mrs. Halamajowa, can't take any of them because we are here.

Her neighbor, Benerowicz, has taken in a Polish refugee family from a neighboring village. This is a large family, with several men and women, and a number of young children. They also brought horses and cattle with them. The horses have been placed into the attic chamber next to the hayloft, which is Benerowicz's territory.

The refugees groom their horses all day and all night. This complicates our lives because we have only the wooden partition to separate us from their animals. What if they discover us? We can hear them calling each other all day long—Karel! Janek! and so forth.

Mrs. Halamajowa is thoroughly upset. She feels that these newcomers are watching her movements all the time. So now she does all the cooking for us late at night, when everyone else is asleep. But she is afraid that her neighbors will wonder about the smoke pouring from her chimney all night long. Instead of bringing us each meal separately, she now brings us our whole day's rations very early in the morning, when it is still dark, because she doesn't want our new neighbors to see her while they are next door to our hayloft grooming their horses. For this reason she also can no longer come to visit with us during the day.

One morning when she brings us our whole day's food supply in a large kettle, she slips and falls from the ladder. She comes to us bent and moaning in pain, hardly able to stand on her feet. "O God," she groans, "what sin have I ever committed that I should suffer so much? I know you're not to blame. You're unhappy, too, because your people are being killed. But what did I need all this trouble for?"

Her words are like knives twisting in our hearts. We know she is right. But what can we do? We are all outlaws, whom everyone wishes to see dead.

Luckily, Mrs. Halamajowa is not badly hurt, but she has to stay in bed for several days. During that time, her daughter Hela looks after us.

Sometimes I wonder whether all the struggle has been worth it. Better to have gone to our death with the rest of the Jews from our town.

In the hayloft, February, 1944

The newspaper reports are good again. The Germans have withdrawn from Lutzk. Their troops have been trapped by the Russians in Kovel and Tarnopol. We no longer need our map to look for the places from which the Germans have retreated. We know the Russians are very close now. Kovel is only about 100 kilometers from here.

Sometimes we look through the crack in the hayloft wall for signs that the Germans are preparing to leave Sokal. We keep asking Mrs. Halamajowa whether she thinks the Germans are about to withdraw from our town.

Finally, one day, she reports that the German occupation authorities are evacuating all the *Volksdeutsche* (ethnic Germans) from Sokal and that the Gestapo has already left. The post office is preparing to close down.

But only a few days later, Mrs. Halamajowa informs us that the Gestapo is back in Sokal, and so are the *Volksdeutsche*. Life in Sokal, she says, is returning to normal. The Ukrainians are killing not only Poles but also many Jews.

Sammy Pass, his wife, their son and daughter Roza hid out in the attic of a Gentile brandy distiller by the name of Gralek. Late one night the Ukrainians broke into Gralek's house and murdered him and his family. Several days later, when they returned to loot the house, the Ukrainians discovered Sammy, his wife and their two children huddled together in the attic. They alerted the Gestapo, who came to the house, took the Passes to some place outside town and shot them.

Mrs. Halamajowa tells us that the Poles who fled to Sokal from other localities to escape the Bandera gangs are leaving again because they are afraid the Ukrainians will take over Sokal also. Mrs. Halamajowa's sister and her family are leaving, too. Mrs. Halamajowa doesn't know what she should do. She says she couldn't abandon us.

The Germans are digging trenches around Sokal; they are rounding up local Poles for the job because there are no German workers left. Poles from Mrs. Halamajowa's neighborhood leave their homes early each morning in search of a place in which to hide during the day so they won't be picked up for labor details. We are afraid they'll come to Mrs. Halamajowa's house in search of a refuge and discover us in her hayloft.

Mrs. Halamajowa tells us that one of her neighbors, a Pole, had two Jewish girls, sisters, hidden at his home. The Pole fled, taking with him the younger of the two girls, who did not look Jewish. The older girl was left behind alone. So she set out for the house of a Gentile she knew. But another Gentile accosted her in the street, yelled "Jew!" grabbed her and handed her over to the Gestapo. "If she would have come to my place, I would have taken her into my home and given her some food," Mrs. Halamajowa concludes her report.

In the hayloft, March, 1944

On March 11, Mrs. Halamajowa comes up to us in the hayloft and hands me a note. She doesn't want to talk because she is afraid she may be overheard. In her note she writes that her neighbor, Benerowicz has told her he'd been suspecting for some time that she has people living in her hayloft. "I want to know just who these people are," he said. So Mrs. Halamajowa wrote us this note, urging us to flee for our lives and not to tell anyone that she had given us shelter.

So this is the end for us. For a year and a half we have been struggling to survive here, and now we are suddenly informed that we might as well give up.

After Mrs. Halamajowa leaves, we discuss what we should do. Perhaps my brother Shmelke should go to Benerowicz at night and tell him, "Yes, it's true. My family is staying in Mrs. Halamajowa's hayloft. But I am heading for the woods to join my partisan unit. If I should hear that something has happened to my family, I will return from the woods with my comrades and get even with you."

But on second thought this sounds foolhardy, almost childish.

We decide on another course of action. Dr. Kindler was a well-known and popular figure in Sokal also among the Gentiles before the war. Mrs. Halamajowa has told us that she hears the Gestapo is on the lookout for him. The local Gentiles know he wasn't killed in the last *Aktion*; there are rumors that he was seen with a unit of partisan fighters. So we decide that Dr. Kindler should try to make an impression on Mr. Benerowicz who doesn't like Jews but hates the Germans just as much and is a fervent Polish patriot. Dr. Kindler should pass himself off as a valiant fighter for the restoration of Polish independence. He should write a letter to Benerowicz, spinning a tall, but entirely plausible, tale. He should say that before the war, he, Kindler, had been living in London, where he had built up a prosperous practice. But when the war broke out, Kindler left everything and flew back to Poland to help defend his country. He was taken prisoner by the Germans, who transferred him to the Warsaw ghetto when they discovered he was Jewish. Kindler managed to escape from there and made his way to Sokal in 1942. When Sokal became *judenrein*, Kindler and his family found shelter at the home of a Pole in Wolyn, but when Kindler heard that the Ukrainians were killing Poles in Sokal, he returned to Sokal to help his Polish fellow citizens there. Mrs. Halamajowa, out of the goodness of her heart, took him into her home and shared her food with him.

Kindler should further write that he worries Mrs. Halamajowa will abandon her home and flee because she is desperately afraid of the Ukrainian gangs. If she runs and the Ukrainians loot her home and discover him there, what does Benerowicz think they will do to him, David Kindler, a known Polish national hero? Surely Benerowicz will agree that a Polish freedom fighter such as Kindler deserves a better fate. Kindler is therefore begging Benerowicz to prevail on Mrs. Halamajowa not to leave her home and to allow him, Kindler, to stay on in her hayloft. He, Kindler, is not without means; so, if God is good and the Germans lose the war, Mrs. Halamajowa can expect a handsome reward from him.

We agree that Kindler should say nothing about the rest of us in his letter to Benerowicz. He should seal the letter and give it to Mrs. Halamajowa, who will see that Benerowicz receives it.

Dr. Kindler agrees to this plan and writes the letter.

Later in the day Mrs. Halamajowa returns to us with a broad grin on her face. "Everything's all right," she says. "You can stay. Benerowicz is leaving." It seems that when Benerowicz received the letter revealing Kindler's "past," he announced to Mrs. Halamajowa that he and his family and the refugees, too, would move out. They will head west, away from the war. He doesn't want trouble from a prominent citizen such as Dr. Kindler, who must have many friends, also in England. At the same time he is afraid that, as Mrs. Halamajowa's neighbor, sharing her house, both the Germans and the Ukrainians will be after him as her accomplice in giving aid and shelter to Jews.

But Mrs. Halamajowa's relative privacy will be short-lived. She has been notified that she will have to open her home to German soldiers. The battle lines are moving closer; there is fighting in Ludmir and Orchev, only 60 kilometers from Sokal. Mrs. Halamajowa says she has seen troops in full battle gear in the streets of Sokal. We can hear gunfire in the distance and, each night, the drone of the heavy bombers overhead.

Two days later we read a *Wehrmacht* communiqué in the newspapers that the towns of Kovel and Dubno have suffered heavy Russian air attacks. So that's where all the heavy bombers have been going.

• • •

Mrs. Halamajowa's daughter Hela has fled westward to escape the advancing Russians, so a niece of Mrs. Halamajowa's has moved in to help in the household. This young woman, the daughter of Mrs. Halamajowa's sister, helps her aunt draw and carry water from the well, but Mrs. Halamajowa does not allow her to do anything else because she must not find out about our existence.

Mrs. Halamajowa's niece has a son, Yurik, who is only one year old and he can't talk yet. He follows his great-aunt wherever she goes. He comes up to us with her each time she brings us food and stares at us with his big baby eyes. He probably doesn't understand what kind of people these could be, sitting in the hayloft all the time and never coming downstairs. He sees Mrs. Halamajowa take food to us, to the chickens and to the pigs. If he can reason that far, he probably thinks that we, too, are some sort of animal species.

• • •

Mrs. Halamajowa often says to us, "Do you think I want to help only you? To me, all good people are the same. I want to help any good and decent person whose life is in danger. I'd even help a German if I thought he deserved it."

• • •

Three German soldiers have moved temporarily into the part of the house where Benerowicz used to live. They have received orders to report to the battlefront near Ludmir and are waiting for transportation. One of the soldiers, a boy of 19, has confided to Mrs. Halamajowa that he really doesn't want to fight for Hitler anymore. He says his mother is Dutch and his father is Catholic. So he has asked Mrs. Halamajowa to give him shelter. He doesn't want to go to the battlefront with the others. Mrs. Halamajowa says she feels sorry for him and has agreed to keep him in her attic. His two comrades wonder what could have happened to him. But they have no time to ask questions, and they are satisfied to leave for the battlefront without him.

We think Mrs. Halamajowa must be joking, but she assures us it's the truth. "I can show you his guns and his munitions belt, if you wish," she says.

In the hayloft, Spring, 1944

Spring is coming. Mrs. Halamajowa is busy tending her garden. She is working even harder than in years past; she wants to make it clear to her neighbors that she has no intention of leaving. She doesn't want to abandon her home and her possessions. Most of the other Poles in Sokal have already left.

• • •

Dr. Kindler's friend, the nurse from the hospital in Sokal, is leaving, too. She has brought Mrs. Halamajowa a package containing the surgical instruments Dr. Kindler left with her. Mrs. Halamajowa gives the package to Dr. Kindler.

Now only about half a dozen Poles are left in all of Sokal: Mrs. Halamajowa, a couple of old beggars who are living in the convent, and one priest from the monastery. The rest are all Ukrainians. The Polish priest often comes to visit Mrs. Halamajowa. Oh, yes, in the house on the left of Mrs. Halamajowa's place there is an ancient Pole. He is 80 years old, deaf, and is coughing all the time. His sons and daughters have fled and left him behind, all alone with his untended garden. The old man sits in his garden all day long, sunning himself and coughing. This is the sort of neighbor we like; he creates no problems for us. We could dance and sing in our hayloft all day and all night, and he'd never hear us. Mrs. Halamajowa, out of pity, takes food to him from time to time.

Our new neighbors to the right, in the place where Benerowicz used to live, are more of a problem. This is a Ukrainian family, all of them apparently pro-German. The family consists of a young couple, plus the wife's mother and younger brother. The husband is a high school teacher; his widowed mother-in-law, Mrs. Metritzky, has come to live with them together with her seventeen-year-old son, Romek. Mrs. Metritzky moved here from the Chelm province where her husband taught elementary school before the war. One night the Poles broke into the Metritzkys' house and hacked Mr. Metritzky to pieces as an act of revenge for what the Ukrainians, pro-Nazis all, were doing to the Poles in Galicia. So the widow moved to Sokal with her son, several wagonloads of cattle and 30 beehives.

Mrs. Metritzky is a very efficient housekeeper; she tends the beehives as well as the garden. We can see her daughter and her son-in-law, the high school teacher, strolling through the garden each day, dressed in the latest fashions. They entertain a lot. Romek Metritzky, a handsome, healthy-looking lad, still goes to school. He brings his friends to the garden to lie in the grass and get a suntan. We seem to recall that we, too, were once human beings. We, too, had money and nice clothes. But today. . . .

This family also has a boarder, a Polish villager with a huge dog. We live in constant fear that the beast might pick up our scent and that would be the end of us.

Mrs. Metritzky and her son Romek have become friendly with the gendarmes. They talk with them in German.

One night there is a little argument between Mrs. Metritzky and Mrs. Halamajowa because Mrs. Metritzky's chickens (she brought those with her, too, from the farm) are ruining Mrs. Halamajowa's garden.

In the hayloft, Spring, 1944

At about two o'clock in the morning we hear footsteps from the courtyard. Later in the morning Mrs. Halamajowa brings us breakfast. She also brings us two flyers crudely printed in Ukrainian. She says she found the flyers pasted on her door. They read, "You'd better leave Ukrainian soil fast because if you don't, we'll execute judgement on you," and so forth. They are signed, "Ukrainian National Council." It doesn't take us long to figure out that these flyers are the work of Romek Metritzky. We tell Mrs. Halamajowa that as soon as we are liberated, we'll take care of this lad. But Mrs. Halamajowa says no, she wouldn't permit us to do anything like that.

This wonderful woman, our guardian angel, is a true saint. Her Ukrainian neighbors are probably aware that she is a Pole, but when they see the young German soldier she is hiding in her home go to the outhouse in the pigsty they think he is a legitimate boarder of hers and they are afraid to bother her because they don't want to get into trouble with the German army.

* * *

The newspapers carry reports of nightly Russian air raids on Lvov, with many casualties. The Russians must be preparing a large-scale offensive. Once the Russians strike, we will be free.

* * *

One day Mrs. Halamajowa comes up to us for a little talk. "Look," she says, "there aren't any more Jews left anywhere. I'd like to have all of you baptized." We do not answer her. We know that there still must be Jews left somewhere in the world.

* * *

The Ukrainians in town are busy digging air raid trenches. Our neighbor, Mrs. Metritzky, is also digging a trench. Her daughter and son-in-law are moving out, to a place on New Street, because the house next to Mrs. Halamajowa's is so close to the River Bug, where fierce fighting will probably take place.

Mrs. Halamajowa brings us a huge barrel and fills it with water. She also brings up a sackful of bread. She wants to make sure we won't go hungry or thirsty if we are caught in the fighting. But for the time being, all is quiet.

June, 1944

No sign of a Russian offensive yet. Mrs. Halamajowa has new lodgers; German troops in retreat, with their armored cars. They don't see the deserter because he is hiding out in Mrs. Halamajowa's attic. The situation is getting dangerous again. Mrs. Halamajowa hasn't come up to us for several days now; she doesn't want the German soldiers to suspect anything.

* * *

These Germans have left, but they have been replaced by other German soldiers. My blood runs cold whenever I hear Mrs. Halamajowa talking in German outside and boasting of her experiences in Germany. "I lived in Germany for 26 years working as a maid for Admiral Land. I still have a plate with a picture of General von Hindenburg." When she starts talking like that, we know that some new German soldiers must have arrived.

• • •

On June 9th, Mrs. Halamajowa informs us that she and the owners of neighboring houses who are still here have received orders to open their homes to retreating German troops. Mrs. Halamajowa only hopes that any soldiers who move in with her won't bring horses, because they would surely put the horses into the pigsty directly below our hayloft. She also hopes that she will not have to take Ukrainians serving in the German army, because they are even more dangerous than the Germans.

At about two o'clock the next morning, we hear the door of Mrs. Halamajowa's house, and the doors of the houses nearby, creak open, and tanks and heavy artillery rumbling into our courtyard.

At daybreak I see, through the crack in the hayloft wall, German soldiers clambering over the roofs and stringing up communications wires. They rip out pieces from doors and roofs of the houses that have been abandoned by fleeing Poles and use them to camouflage the bunkers and trenches they are building.

In one of the trenches a cannon is being installed, guarded by a German soldier in full battle dress. The Germans seem to be digging in for a long stay. Fear has returned to our hayloft. What if one of the German soldiers should climb the roof of our hayloft from the outside, tear off a piece to use as camouflage, and discover us?

The Germans are installing telephones on the roofs of the houses. We quickly seal every crack and opening in the roof of our hayloft. This shuts out all the daylight. In the pitch darkness we huddle together in the straw and pull our blankets over our heads.

• • •

The following afternoon, Mrs. Halamajowa comes up to us at the usual time, but without any food. She tosses the newspaper to us and says, "You'd better pray very diligently to your God because we are all lost. The Germans are moving in."

The newspaper is an army newspaper. All the regular newspapers in Lvov, the nearest city, have ceased publication.

We ask Mrs. Halamajowa to make sure she is frequently seen around her house and in her garden so the Germans shouldn't think her house has been abandoned. If they see that the house is occupied, they probably will not try to enter our hayloft in search of more camouflage material.

From whom, we ask Mrs. Halamajowa, did she get the newspaper? She says she got it from some German soldiers who have moved into her house. I open the newspaper. The headlines say that the Allies have opened a second front in France on June 6. This is the second front for which so many Jews have been waiting so long and which so many of them did not live to see. We have lived to see it, but there can be no joy for us because we are now surrounded by Germans.

That evening Mrs. Halamajowa brings us some food. She says her house is packed with German troops, all of them officers. Now she has to cook for them, too.

The next day the Germans are out in full force again, digging trenches. The guard in full battle gear is also back, guarding the cannon in the trench. Another day of fear and apprehension for us.

On the third day, it's the same story all over again.

In the afternoon of the fourth day, we hear the German soldiers going through their drill in the courtyard. One voice—apparently an officer—announces, "We're leaving, men." Someone asks him, "Where are we headed?" The officer replies, "My good man, the world is a big place." This sounds encouraging but how do we know that the Germans are really leaving?

In the evening, Mrs. Halamajowa comes to us and tells us that the Germans are indeed leaving. One young German volunteer has explained to her that he and the other soldiers were transferred to this area from France, but now that the Allies have opened a second front, they are eager to return to France as soon as possible.

At one o'clock in the morning, we hear a lot of noise outside: motors starting, heavy doors opening and military vehicles driving away. I tell Dr. Kindler that if we were able to survive those days of pure hell, we'll also live to see the end of the war.

In the hayloft, late June, 1944

This morning the trenches the Germans dug are empty. The cannon is also gone. All is quiet again. We open a crack in the hayloft wall to see what is going on outside.

* * *

The Germans have come back to our street and to Mrs. Halamajowa's house. This time, it's a construction battalion who are building a bridge across the River Bug. But these Germans aren't such a threat to us because they leave for their work early in the morning and don't return until after dark.

Sokal is full of German troops. When I look out through the crack in the hayloft wall, I can see a huge swastika flag waving from the roof of a large building on the main highway. Mrs. Halamajowa says that the Germans have taken over this building as their staff headquarters. The lawn around the building is covered with German soldiers and military vehicles, and drill is held every day.

* * *

Mrs. Halamajowa has more disquieting news for us. There are rumors that the entire civilian population of Sokal will be evacuated because heavy fighting is expected on the banks of the River Bug. She says she doesn't know what we should do if this happens and she has to leave her house. She suggests that the four children—the two Kindler boys, my son Chaim and my sister Leah's Feyge Chashe— should learn the Lord's Prayer and a couple of German hymns so that if we have to flee for our lives, they can pass as Christians. She has bought peasant kerchiefs for our women so they should look as Gentile as possible and no one should recognize them.

* * *

For several days now, planes have been cruising overhead. At first glance they look like German planes. Our neighbors (those that are still here) run for shelter in the trenches left behind by the German soldiers. However, we can soon tell from the markings that he planes are not German but Russian.

* * *

The last battle has begun. At noon the shooting begins; our hayloft is shaking. We can see people racing through the streets as if they have gone crazy. The long-awaited final act of this horrible drama is about to start. Mrs. Halamajowa tells us that Sokal's railroad station has received a direct hit in an air raid and that a train standing in the station was blown up. There are many dead and wounded. The wounded have been taken to the hospital.

In the hayloft, Sunday, July 15, 1944

We hear the steady drone of wave after wave of airplanes over-head. This must be the start of the long-awaited all-out Russian attack.

In the hayloft, Saturday, July 16, 1944

We hear the rumble of wheels from the highway. These are military vehicles filled with German soldiers, apparently in full retreat.

In the hayloft, Monday, July 17, 1944

This morning Mrs. Halamajowa tells us that the Ukrainians are fleeing from Sokal with their horses and cattle. Russian planes appear overhead. The anti-aircraft battery near the church is in operation. The Soviet bombers are flying low. This is a battle of bombs and machine guns. Our hayloft is shaking. All our remaining neighbors have taken to the trenches.

Our children have wrapped themselves in their blankets. Only Mrs. Halamajowa is bustling about happily because she knows the war will be over soon and she'll get the reward I promised her: I'll make her the sole owner of the house in which she is living.

We are happy, too. We're not afraid of the shooting and the shelling. We wonder aloud who among the Jews in Sokal might still be alive. Dr. Kindler mentions the names of people he knows, including several doctors and their families, who he thinks will have survived the *Aktion* with forged Aryan documents.

I say that the Jewish intelligentsia in Sokal has lost out on every count. Even if they survive, they have lost themselves because most of them were hell-bent on assimilation.

In the hayloft, Tuesday, July 18, 1944

The bombs are falling again. A German plane has been shot down on the banks of the River Bug where the cattle usually graze.

Mrs. Halamajowa reports that the Russians have occupied the towns of Spasow and Luchitz, just 20 kilometers from Sokal. She says the Germans are in full retreat. I ask Mrs. Halamajowa to let us know as soon as she sees fire on the wooden bridge across the River Bug, which is only 300 yards from her garden. "When the Germans set fire to the bridge," I explain to the others, "it'll be a sign that they have decided to abandon Sokal."

In the hayloft, Wednesday, July 19, 1944

At two in the morning the machine guns start up again. At three A.M. Mrs. Halamajowa appears and informs us that the bridge is on fire. Soon, very soon, we'll be able to leave the hayloft. It's already safe, I think, to make a little noise. For the first time in 21 months I let my feet touch a bare spot on the floor of the hayloft.

At five A.M. Mrs. Halamajowa announces that Russian patrols already appeared in Sokal. Russian troops are crossing the River Bug. The Germans are shelling Sokal from the town of Opiksk, three kilometers away. The noise is earsplitting. The gunfire is aimed at the Tartakow highway to stop the advancing Russian troops from using it. Mrs. Halamajowa says the town is virtually in ruins from the shelling.

Mrs. Halamajowa brings us noodles and enough meat to last for several days, but we aren't interested in food just now. We have been making plans for leaving the hayloft and going home, but we decide we can't venture into the town as yet because of all the shooting.

In the afternoon the shooting subsides a little. Only now do we learn that Mrs. Halamajowa is sheltering a Jewish family of three in the cellar of her own house: my friend Joshua Kram, his wife and his child. Mrs. Halamajowa brings the Krams up to us in the hayloft; there is hugging and kissing all around.

Kram, who is a housepainter, tells us how he and his family survived. Not long after the Germans took Sokal, he painted Mrs. Halamajowa's living room. On that occasion he gave Mrs. Halamajowa some money and asked her whether she would be willing to shelter him and his wife if there was an *Aktion*. Her reply had been, "Why not?" When Sokal was declared *judenrein*, Kram was in a labor camp outside the ghetto where the Germans kept skilled Jewish workers day and night to make sure they would not be caught in an *Aktion*. Mrs. Kram and their child were in a bunker inside the ghetto; since they could contribute nothing to the Nazi war effort, their lives were worth nothing. From time to time, Kram would sneak out of the camp and bring food to his family in the ghetto.

Two weeks after the final *Aktion*, the Jewish workers in the labor camp were stripped down to their underwear, piled into two trucks and driven to a place outside the city to be shot. Kram jumped from the truck half naked, right in front of the ditch that had been dug as a mass grave for the victims. The Germans took aim at him but he escaped, hiding amidst the tall grain in the fields

That night he entered the ghetto, went to the bunker where his wife and child were hiding, smuggled the two of them out of the ghetto under cover of darkness, and took them straight to Mrs. Halamajowa's house. Mrs. Halamajowa had just finished cutting a hole in her kitchen floor directly above her cellar when the Krams arrived, so she was ready for them. After the Krams had gone down to the cellar by way of a ladder, Mrs. Halamajowa covered the hole with floor boards and placed a table on top of the boards.

• • •

Mrs. Halamajowa asks Dr. Kindler whether he has a spare suit for the young German deserter who is still hiding in her attic, so the Russians will not catch him in his German uniform. Dr. Kindler gives her one of his suits.

• • •

We talk again about going home. Mrs. Halamajowa says she doesn't want any of the Ukrainian anti-Semites in her street to see us leave her house. But we don't see a soul outside. The time has come for us to go home.

Mrs. Halamajowa gives us 300 zlotys and another 200 to the Kindlers so we should have a little cash to buy whatever we may need.

On Wednesday, July 19, 1944, at three P.M., Mrs. Halamajowa bids farewell to the 15 Jews who owe her their survival: my mother, my wife, our son Chaim, myself, our sisters Leah and Yitte, Leah's daughter Feyge Chashe, my brother Shmelke, the four Kindlers and the three Krams. She walks with us a little part of the way. We pass through the gardens in the back of the neighboring houses. Each of us is carrying a package with some of the things we brought with us to Mrs. Halamajowa's hayloft. We try to walk without stopping, but our legs won't carry us. Every step hurts. After so many months of virtual immobility in incredibly cramped quarters, we have forgotten how to walk.

VI

Liberation—July 1944–May 1945

Sokal, Wednesday, July 19, 1944

As we come closer to our homes, we see no civilians in the streets, only long lines of Russian soldiers marching single file, with guns and steel helmets. They are wearing ponchos over their uniforms because it is raining. We pass wagons loaded with Russian wounded, pulled by large dogs.

A Russian officer stops in his tracks, points his gun at us and asks in Russian where we are going. I tell him, also in Russian, that we are Jews, that we have been hiding for almost two years, and that we are now going home.

"Did you say you're Jewish?" the Russian officer exclaims in Yiddish. So this Russian army officer is Jewish! I therefore think it's safe to ask him a question. Should we go to our homes in Sokal or should we keep going someplace further east? Does he think the Germans may come back and chase the Russians out of Sokal? The officer simply replies, again in Yiddish, "Stay here in Sokal." He says he hasn't time to talk anymore because he and his men have to get on with the fighting.

We keep walking, or better crawling, along. After two years spent lying or crouching in the hayloft, our bodies are stiff. Dr. Kindler is bent almost double, leaning on a stick he has picked up somewhere.

The houses we pass show the traces of battle, but there are people inside. One man rushes out, yelling, "Dr. Kindler! Help me!" His head is bandaged with rags. He says he was hit by a stray bullet. Dr. Kindler examines him; the wound is only superficial. Dr. Kindler takes a clean bandage from his medical bag and dresses the wound. Then we move on.

The Kindlers bid us farewell and go off to their house. My house is only about one kilometer from Mrs. Halamajowa's place, but it takes our family two hours to get there.

When we finally arrive, we find our entire house was taken over by the post office as temporary headquarters for its technical division.

But now all the personnel is gone. I find a few pieces of furniture that we left behind when we moved into the ghetto.

We clear away all the postal equipment. My mother pulls a *mezuzah* from her bag. It is the *mezuzah* she removed from her own home when she and my father moved into the ghetto; she has carried it with her all this time. Now she produces a pair of nails (wherever did she find them?) and firmly fastens the *mezuzah* to our doorpost.

We look around. Are we still alive, or is this only a wishful daydream?

Suddenly a loud explosion outside blows our doors and window slats wide open. There is a smell of smoke. We run outside. The house where our neighbor, Boschwitzer, used to live, has been hit by a hand grenade. We make for our cellar to take cover in case another grenade comes flying. Only the day before, when the shooting went on nonstop, we lay in Mrs. Halamajowa's hayloft and laughed because we simply didn't care what happened to us as long as the Germans got what they deserved. But now we are free, and we want to remain alive.

We stay in our cellar for a while. Since we hear no more explosions outside, we finally go upstairs.

You hardly see anyone on the street. The few miserable Ukrainians who haven't run away seem to be hiding in the cellars of their homes. They are afraid of the Russians.

Russian soldiers enter our home and question us in minute detail. They seem surprised to find us here. A Russian major talks to us in a broken Yiddish. He says he has come all the way from Moscow with the Red Army without ever seeing a Jew—until now. He leaves, but he soon returns with several other Russian officers. They all stare at this wonder of wonders—Jews, real Jews!

Chaim and Feyge Chashe don't even know how to talk above a whisper. They speak in such low voices that nobody understands them.

A few Polish Gentiles come by. They ask us where we have been all this time. We answer that we were hiding out in the woods.

In the evening someone unlocks the door of a building only three doors away from my home. The Germans used the building as a warehouse. People rush in and take out as much food as they can carry. We pick up a few sacks of unsifted flour and a jar of marmalade.

Our beds are gone, but we have our blankets from the hayloft. That night we sleep in our own home for the first time in almost two years.

Sokal, Thursday, July 20, 1944

Today we sit in our courtyard, enjoying the fresh air. Poles and Russian soldiers stop to get a good look at us. They even take pictures. Dr. Kindler comes over for a visit from his house, which he found "in shamble, but habitable, at least for the present," as he put it. Old Dr. Macziewicz, a Ukrainian, appears. He says he is the only doctor left in Sokal. "Let's live together as brothers," he says to Dr. Kindler. Two years ago he wouldn't even have looked at a Jew. When a Jew greeted him, he pointedly ignored him, and now he wants to live with as a brother. When the Germans came to Sokal, Macziewicz suggested that Kindler take poison; now he claims he's happy that Kindler is still alive.

Mrs. Halamajowa pays us a call. She sits down on a bench in our courtyard. She says she is very happy to see us in our home again. She impresses on us that she doesn't want it known that she hid us in her hayloft. The Poles in town, she says, don't like people who put themselves out to help Jews.

•　•　•

Liszka, the daughter of Yankel Eimer, a friend of ours, appears with two other girls. After the hugging and kissing, Liszka tells us how she survived: she was hidden at the home of a woman who used to work as a maid in her family.

Shmelke and I explore the courtyard to look for things we could use to set up housekeeping. We have returned home with very little more than the clothes on our backs. We inspect the neighboring courtyard of what was once the post office building, and there we come upon an odd-looking structure about 20 meters long, right in the middle of the courtyard. The Germans must have put it up as a stable for their horses, says Shmelke. It must have sustained a direct hit because there is a deep bomb crater next to it, and half of the structure is in ruins.

We enter the undamaged half of this structure and stand rooted to the spot in shock and amazement. There is a shelf piled high with Torah scrolls. Once upon a time, when they were new, these scrolls, in keeping with time-honored custom, were brought into the synagogue beneath a canopy, with music and dancing, and then solemnly installed into the Holy Ark. Today they lie in the ruins of a horses' stable. Shmelke and I tenderly pick up the scrolls, one by one, and carry them into my house. There are altogether 13 scrolls.

I hear someone calling my name. A group of armed Russian soldiers are half-leading, half-shoving one Ukrainian. I remember this Ukrainian; he used to work as a postal clerk for the Germans, but that's all I really know about him. One of the Russian soldiers, an officer, enters my house and leads me into my living room. "Do you know this man?" he asks, pointing to the Ukrainian. "What kind of work was he doing for the Germans? Has he ever harmed anybody?" I can't answer the last question, because I really do not know.

The Russian officer turns out to be Jewish. He explains he belongs to the "fighting NKVD," the branch of the Communist secret police who follow the advancing Soviet troops to interrogate the local civilian populace and deal with Nazi collaborators. He says to me in Yiddish, "If you know of anyone who murdered a Jew, turn him over to me and I'll deal with him."

We probably won't get to see any big-time murderers because they surely have fled with the retreating Germans. The small fry must be hiding in the church, where they expect to be safe.

The Russian soldiers leave. But a few hours later the Jewish NKVD officer is back. "Tell me where those gangsters are!" he commands. I answer that perhaps by tomorrow, I'll have found a few. He replies, "Too bad. We won't be here anymore tomorrow; we're advancing with the fighting troops."

In the evening, two more survivors appear: the Bryh brothers. They tell us they were hidden at the home of a Pole and later took to the woods.

Tomorrow, Friday, July 21, 1944, will be our third day of freedom.

Sokal, late July, 1944

I have begun to venture out a little, but never very far from my house because I still don't feel strong enough to see the homes of my relatives and friends who are gone.

The house of my neighbor, Shlomo Schuman, the tavernkeeper, is intact, but no one is inside. No one at all.

On Monday, July 24, I visit the marketplace. I meet Riczki, Schuman's old Polish servant. He says he hardly ever leaves his home nowadays. He still mourns the Schumans. He looked after them even during the German occupation. He tells me that after the final *Aktion* in which Shlomo was deported (his wife, Altshe, had the "luxury" of dying in her own bed, of typhoid fever), the Schumans' son-in-law,

Milty Rosenblatt and Rosenblatt's son, Shabse, managed to hide in the attic of their house for five weeks. He, Riczki, used to bring them food. But eventually they were discovered and reported to the Gestapo.

Where are the coachmen with the hansom cabs that once stood in the marketplace, close to Schuman's house, waiting for passengers? The marketplace is as silent as a graveyard.

I don't feel like going any further. I have had enough for the day. As I reach the entrance of my house, two people, bent over and leaning heavily on canes, come toward me. They seem happy to see me, but I am not sure who they are. I look at them more closely, and I finally recognize them. They are the son and daughter of my friend Zyshe. They were hidden in the home of a Gentile in a neighboring village.

A pitiful figure comes into view—in rags, unshaven, his face a mass of running sores. He is Mendel Igel of Doroczyn. He survived in Doroczyn, sheltered at the home of a Pole. His sister, who went into hiding at the home of another Gentile, was not so fortunate. A gang of Poles discovered her and took her to Gestapo headquarters. She knew one of the Poles; he used to do business with her parents before the war. So she asked him, "Genek, why do you want to kill me?" and Genek replied, "Don't expect me to get you out of this; you're just another damned Jew-girl."

Moshe Daks, a leader in our religious Zionist organization before the war, comes by with his wife. They were sheltered at the home of a Gentile in Tartakow.

The next survivors I meet are the Schiffenbauers—Leibush, with his wife and one child. Before the war he was the manager of a large estate. The Schiffenbauers, too, survived at the home of a Gentile acquaintance. They also had another child, a daughter who would be twelve now, but she is gone. Three months before the liberation, the man at whose home the Schiffenbauers had taken shelter told them that he wouldn't be able to keep them in his house much longer. The twelve-year-old girl said to him, "That's all right. I'll leave and go somewhere else, so you'll have one less person to worry about." She left and that was the last her parents saw of her. They are sure she is dead.

Sokal, August 1944

My brother Shmelke and I are standing in front of my house. A young girl, barefoot, with a package under her arm, walks toward us.

"Would you know where the Schiffenbauers are living?" she asks us in Ukrainian. "Could you be their daughter?" I ask her in Yiddish. She answers yes, she is. Shmelke runs to tell the Schiffenbauers that their daughter has come back. The girl survived by passing as a Gentile and tending to the sheep of a peasant.

• • •

My home has become the center for Jewish survivors who come to Sokal from neighboring localities to look for relatives and friends. They are directed to my house, where they get a proper meal, prepared from groceries I have been taking from the former German warehouse.

Five boys from Tartakow have come to town. They escaped from a concentration camp in Zborow the day before all the inmates were incinerated. They hid in the woods for 13 months. They look like wild animals—unshaven, barefoot, their feet and legs swollen. They are clothed in rags that cling to their filthy bodies.

Rozsa Leimsieder, a friend of my sister Yitte, has also come back. She was sheltered at the home of a Ukrainian girlfriend. Hersh Klar, of the Jewish police, and his wife have survived because a Pole in the Hrubieszow district kept them in his home.

The two daughters of Nachman Lentz are back. One of them is married, with a child. The other is single. Their father was the town *shlepper*, a simple fellow who worked at odd jobs as a farmhand. We called him "Laughing Nachman" because he was always in a good mood. His two daughters have survived by passing as Gentiles, moving from village to village working on farms.

• • •

We are gradually settling down at home. Dr. Kindler and his family, who now consider their old home unhabitable, have moved in with the Bryh brothers. We have asked every Jewish family that has returned to its old home in Sokal to take in survivors whose homes have been destroyed or who have come to Sokal from other localities.

We go to the former Gestapo headquarters and take some of the furniture from there. It's all furniture stolen from Jewish homes. We also enter houses abandoned by the Ukrainians and help ourselves to any food and household utensils we find there.

• • •

One Sunday I finally work up the courage to visit the ghetto. I gather a group of Jews to go with me and we are on our way.

We come to the entrance of the ghetto. The ruins of the guard-house (only one wall and the chimney are left) are topped by a sign stating in large Russian letters that this is a monument to the destructing wrought by the "wild beasts."

We turn into the Street of the Synagogues.* Ruins everywhere. The cobbled streets have been washed clean by a recent summer rainstorm. No one seems to have set foot on them for some time. Grass is sprouting between the cobblestones. We pass the *genizah,* the place where pious worshippers once left holy books that were torn and could no longer be used for prayer and study. Such books were not discarded but were gathered in the *genizah* and buried.

We come to the site where the rabbi's house once stood. Nothing is left of the house. It seems that even the ruins have been broken up and the stones removed by souvenir hunters.

The three synagogue buildings are still standing, but they are empty shells. The inside of each synagogue has been gutted and desecrated. The *Beth Medrash* has a sign reading, "German Grain Warehouse." We go inside. There are neither benches or tables. The cantor's stand and the Holy Ark are gone. Only the steps that led to the Ark have remained. These are the very steps from which our cantor, Leizer Melammed, honored prominent congregants with the traditional melodious call to read from the Torah on *Simhat Torah,* the Rejoicing of the Law.** The steps that led to the Torah reading table are still there, and so are the four iron columns that graced each corner of the table. But the fine Jews who studied and prayed in this synagogue are no more.

I stand in silence, unable to speak. I can almost see them before my eyes, my relatives and friends, even the places where they sat at study and prayer. And I can also picture them going to their deaths.

We leave the *Beth Medrash* and stand quietly in the street. We remember the mood of solemn awe that pervaded this street just before the services on Yom Kippur Eve, the holiest day of the Jewish year. I

---

* This street, part of the old Jewish section of Sokal, was incorporated into the ghetto area by the *Judenrat* and the Gestapo when they set up the ghetto.

** The joyous festival immediately following the fall holiday, Sukkoth, when the Pentateuchal reading cycle is completed with the completion of the Book of Deuteronomy and immediately resumed with the opening verses of Genesis.

can almost see women hurrying to visit the rabbi shortly before the services begin, to listen to the penitential sermon he has prepared especially for them. I can picture the rabbi walking swiftly to the synagogue with his entourage, the rabbi, majestic in his white gown and yarmulka and his heirloom tallith.

The well outside the *Beth Medrash* is still there, but the Jewish children who once pumped water from it are gone.

We move to the Tailor's Synagogue where the working people used to pray. We enter the vestibule. The first sight that meets our eyes is a pile of artificial fertilizer and a huge scale. With great difficulty we push open the door that divides the vestibule from the sanctuary. The sanctuary has been stripped bare. The Ark has survived, only because it is not a separate piece of furniture but has been built into the eastern wall. I can almost see the working people and the "enlightened" Jews who considered themselves more broad-minded and cultured than the rest, standing and swaying at their prayers. I can hear Leib, the sexton, reciting the kiddush over the wine after the Friday night service in his tremulous stammer.

From the Tailor's Synagogue we go to the *klaus* of the Husyatin Hasidim. This building, too, has somehow remained standing amidst the ruins of the houses that once surrounded it. Here, again, a sign on the door: "German Grain Warehouse." The interior is gutted. I remember the festively-dressed men and women who once filled this hall, and the cantor, Reb Meir Leib Glaser, with his moving rendition of the prayers. My friends and I used to go to this synagogue from time to time, especially to hear Reb Meir chant *Musaf*, the late morning service on Sabbaths and festivals. Where is Reb Meir now, and where are my friends? Vanished, as if they had never been. . . .

Leaving the synagogues behind us, we come to Konotop Street. Not a trace is left of the wooden houses that once stood there. We can still see remnants of the bunkers in which Jews took shelter at the end. Every bit of ground has been dug up by looters in search of money and possessions left behind by the Jews.

The sidewalks are overgrown with grass. Scattered here and there we find remnants of holy books, their pages slashed and tattered. I trip over an object. it is a human skull with some hair still on it.

The public steam bath where Jews used to gather for a *shvitz* is still here, but its walls are cold and dry. The threshold is covered with moss.

A few more Jews have come to Sokal. Among them is a woman from Orniew with a little boy. She hid in the woods. Her toes were frozen. She amputated them herself with a knife, cutting off the gangrenous toes and then bandaging her mutilated foot with rags. Another new arrival is a woman from Stanyatin, with her little daughter. The two hid out for some time at the home of a Gentile and later in the woods. Her older child, a boy, died in her arms of cold and starvation.

• • •

The handful of Jews in Sokal don't have enough to eat. They pick vegetables from gardens formerly owned by Jews but now in the hands of Gentiles. The Gentiles report the thefts to the Soviets. The Soviet authorities ask the Jews why they did it, but they make no attempt to prosecute or punish them.

• • •

Dr. Kindler has given us three gold coins to sell so we should have some cash to live on. Dr. Kindler is the only Jewish survivor here who is already making a living of sorts. Patients are coming to him from all over. None of them has any cash, but they bring him chickens, flour or butter in payment for his services. These can be kept or sold on the black market. Dr. Kindler gives the families of all his Jewish patients a chicken for the Sabbath.

Mrs. Metritzky, Mrs. Halamajowa's former neighbor, apparently wants to convince us, and everyone else in town, especially the Jews and the Soviet authorities, that she never had any Nazi sympathies. She brings me a liter of milk, a piece of butter and a little honey from her beehives each day, all on credit. I'll pay her when I have the money. It seems that she is doing this at the suggestion of Mrs. Halamajowa who, she now appears to think, is an ethnic German. Mrs. Metritzky sees that Mrs. Halamajowa and we are good friends, but she doesn't suspect the reason.

• • •

I ask two of our friends to go with me to what was once the garden of my sister Leah's father-in-law, Shmuel Letzter, to look for the furs we buried there in 1942. Shmuel, his wife and his children are gone. His son Eli, my sister Leah's husband, was shot at the very beginning; the others perished later. The Letzters' house is partially destroyed. The garden fence has been removed and the garden dug up, apparently by Polish or Ukrainian looters.

Finally, after half a day's digging, we find the milk cans with our good furs still inside. We have a strong feeling that the neighbors have been watching us and are wishing they discovered the furs before we got there.

The very next day rumors are rife that my friends and I have dug up a canful of gold coins.

• • •

Almost a month has gone by since our liberation. We are gathering all the Jewish survivors in Sokal, young and old, for a pilgrimage to the mass graves on the outskirts of town where the Jews shot by the Nazis are buried.

We march along the Tartakow highway. All the houses have bombed and shelled to rubble and the streets are broken up. We ourselves look like a procession of walking wounded.

We pass long lines of wagons piled high with wounded Russian soldiers from the battlefront. The poor fellows are moaning with pain. They are staring at us as if they were wondering what our procession is all about. But we, the Jews, and those Russians are victims of the same murderers.

We walk past the place where the brick factory once stood. All the brick factories around Sokal have been burned to the ground and the smokestacks blown up by land mines.

As we continue on our way, we see the aftermath of war; wrecked military vehicles and bullet-riddled tanks. We are looking for the mass graves. We have with us one woman who says she knows the way to the biggest one. She says she has already visited it with a Gentile, who told her, "This is where all the Jews of Sokal are buried." So now she guides us to several rows of long, low mounds, covered with grass. This is the place where, the woman says, four thousand Jews were shot and buried. Beneath this ground lies a community of Jews that began hundreds of years ago. Here the history of this community has come to an abrupt end. We all weep bitterly as we recite the prayer *El Maleh Rachamim* (God Full of Compassion) and the Mourner's Kaddish.

My brother Shmelke and the women in our family want to know where the 400 martyrs shot by the Germans in November, 1941 are buried, for among those dead is my brother-in-law Eli Letzter. One of the men in our group thinks he knows where that mass grave must be. "We should pass it on our way back into town," he tells me. We find the place and here, too, we tearfully recite *El Maleh Rachamim* and the

Kaddish. Feyge Chashe, Eli's child, is not with us. She is only six years old.

We trudge back to town in silence. No one utters a word. We feel the tragedy of our people wherever we go. As you walk through certain streets you realize to your horror that you are walking on ancient headstones from an old Jewish cemetery. The Germans pulled out the headstones and ordered Jewish slave laborers to repave the streets with them. The stones show Hebrew dates and epitaphs hundreds of years old.

• • •

For us, Sokal is one huge graveyard. You enter a Jewish store and find the place abandoned. The Ukrainians who moved in after the original Jewish owners were deported have fled. The floor is littered with fragments of holy books, huge Talmudic folios with pages torn out for use as wrapping paper. You go into a cobbler's shop and see that the cobbler has been using sheets of parchment from Torah scrolls to make insoles. . . .

• • •

We who have survived want to make certain that orphaned Jewish children who were sheltered at the homes of Gentiles will not be lost to the Jewish people.

I am told that a young boy has been seen on Swetlowa Street with a crowd of Gentiles. I immediately go to find out who he is. He says his name if Yoshe Zigmont, and that he is twelve years old. He escaped from the ghetto with his mother during the last *Aktion.* They fled to Wolyn, where they were seized by Ukrainian Bandera gangsters. The Ukrainians tossed his mother into a well but Yoshe escaped. A peasant from a nearby village took him to his home, fed and sheltered him and taught him the Baptist faith. So now, after the liberation, Yoshe has returned to Sokal with a Baptist prayer book and is living with a Gentile family, former neighbors of his parents, on Swetlowa Street.

I urge him to come and live with us Jews instead and return to the religion of h is parents. Several days later he really does come to us. Dr. Kindler takes him into his home. Yoshe begins to go to the synagogue regularly with Dr. Kindler's two sons. Before long he has forgotten all about the Baptist faith and had become a Jew again.

A Ukrainian woman from Wolyn turns up in Sokal with a twelve-year-old Jewish girl in tow. The girl is from Hordilovich. She was locked up in a ghetto but escaped and returned to her home town. Since she couldn't find a Gentile willing to give her shelter, she crossed the River Bug and eventually landed in Wolyn. The Ukrainian woman who had no children of her own, took the Jewish girl into her home. The woman's husband, leader of a Bandera gang, has been arrested by the Russians and is now in prison in Sokal. In order to get her husband released, the woman has come here with the Jewish girl as evidence of her husband's innocence. Look, he even allowed her to rescue a Jewish child!

When she learns that her story won't get her husband out of prison, she wants to go home to Wolyn with the girl. But we Jews take the girl from her and the woman has to go home alone. We discover that one of the survivors who has returned to Sokal is related to the girl. He gladly agrees to take her into his home, and one more child is saved for her people. [*This girl eventually settled in Israel, had six children and now is the grandmother of 18.*]

Mrs. Halamajowa comes to visit us every day, bringing us groceries that the Kindlers are sending her daily. "I have plenty of food," she says to my wife, Chana. "Why don't we share whatever the Kindlers send me?"

The young German deserter is still at her home, hiding in the attic. I urge her to let us turn him over to the Soviet authorities. But she refuses to do that; she says it would be cruel, because the Russians would probably execute him as a German spy. She wants to keep the boy hidden at her home until the war is officially ended, This irks me. Besides, I'm worried that she will get into trouble if the Russians find a German soldier in her house. Dr. Kindler, the housepainter Kram and I decide that, together, we should kidnap the German and hand him over to the Russians. I am sure that, in the end, Mrs. Halamajowa will realize that we did this for her own good.

But Mrs. Kindler insists on getting into the act. She says, "It isn't right for a public figure like my husband, a well-known doctor, to become involved in such matters. Why don't the two of you do it without him?" But Kram and I don't want to act without Dr. Kindler. During the next few days we pay several visits to Kindler's house to discuss the plan, but Mrs. Kindler will not let her husband go with us to kidnap the German deserter. So we decide to leave the young German where he is—at least for the present.

• • •

Meanwhile, a military commission from Moscow has arrived in Sokal to inspect the Jewish mass graves. This commission, which consists of five high-ranking officers, has sent for us Jews and questioned us in detail. They ask us for the names of all the Gestapo men who were stationed in Sokal during the German occupation. They also ask us to take them to the mass graves. They dig up the graves and take pictures. After counting the bodies they have found, they say they want to put up a fence around the area and eventually build a monument there.

The NKVD has given orders that every person in Sokal must report to them in order to receive an identification document they call *spravka*. We Jews promptly go to get our *spravka*.

• • •

One morning there is a knock on the door of our house. I look down from an upstairs window and see Russian soldiers, armed to the teeth. I go downstairs and open the door for them.

The Russians enter and order me to show them my identification papers. When they see that we are Jewish, they make only a cursory inspection of our house and then leave without a word. But we know what is going on: the Russians are searching every home in town for Nazi collaborators. "Our friend, Mrs. Halamajowa, will be in deep trouble if the Russians find that German boy in her attic," I say to Shmelke that evening. "Let's go to her and warn her." But it's too late in the day for us to go because the curfew is already in force and will last until six o'clock the next morning.

Moments after six the next morning, Shmelke and I rush to Mrs. Halamajowa's place, but we arrive there only just in time to see Russian soldiers take her away. She is as pale as a ghost. When she sees us she becomes a little calmer. The Russians say they are taking her to the building where the Soviet authorities have set up their military headquarters. Shmelke and I follow them and ask to see the military investigator.

The investigator, an officer with the rank of captain, turns out to be Jewish. He explains that Mrs. Halamajowa has been placed under arrest for having given shelter to a German spy. We take the captain to our house and tell him the whole story of how Mrs. Halamajowa saved our lives by giving us shelter in her hayloft. We also assure him that the young German soldier is not a Nazi spy but in fact a deserter from the *Wehrmacht*.

It's too late, the captain replies. Mrs. Halamajowa's case has already been entered in the official record, so he has to hand her over to the NKVD. However, he agrees to put in a good word for her.

All the 15 of us whom Mrs. Halamajowa saved, including the five children (the Kindler boys, Chaim, Feyge Chashe and the Krams' child), go together to NKVD headquarters to plead for her release, but it doesn't help. We ask to speak to the military commission that came here from Moscow to inspect the mass graves. At that point we hear a Russian officer from the commission say, "They're hanging a woman today for hiding a German spy in her attic." I tell the Russian that this is the woman about whom we want to talk to the commission. We explain who Mrs. Halamajowa is, and what she did for us. They reply that this is a good story, but that Mrs. Halamajowa had two weeks in which to report the presence of an enemy soldier in her house but had failed to do so. "If she'd have reported him," the chief investigator concludes, "we'd have told her, 'Thank you very much,' and that would have been all. But now, since she didn't report him, and we discovered him hiding out in her attic. . . ."

We produce some of the notes Mrs. Halamajowa passed to us in her hayloft when she was afraid to speak, notes telling us about her fervent prayers that God might help us and let the Russians come soon to set us free. We also explain once again that the young German is definitely not a Nazi spy but just a cowardly deserter.

We spend the rest of the day, without a thought for food pleading with the Russians on Mrs. Halamajowa's behalf. Finally, in the evening, Mrs. Halamajowa is pronounced not guilty and released. We all crowd around her hugging and kissing her.

The next day Shmelke goes to Mrs. Halamajowa's house. When he arrives there, he finds the place surrounded by NKVD men. When Shmelke asks them what they want from Mrs. Halamajowa, they reply that apparently she isn't in, but they are waiting for her because she is wanted for interrogation.

Shmelke runs home to tell me. By a happy accident, he finds Mrs. Halamajowa sitting in our living room on one of her daily visits.

After a brief discussion we decide that, in view of the Russians' unpredictable behavior, it is not safe for Mrs. Halamajowa to remain in Sokal. She should leave immediately and go to her daughter Hela, who fled west from the advancing Russian forces and is now living in Lanzut. Sokal is under Soviet occupation , but Lanzut has become part of the newly established free Polish Republic. There our Mrs. Halamajowa will be safe.

We inform Dr. Kindler, who comes rushing to our house with money and food for the trip, and also a bottle of whiskey from which she can offer drinks in return for lifts on military vehicles.

We bid farewell and send Shmelke with her to escort her as far as the border between the Soviet-occupied area and independent Poland. She leaves us with only the clothes on her back, her handbag (containing, among other things, the money from Dr. Kindler), and a satchel into which we have placed the food and the whiskey.

• • •

The Russians have confiscated Mrs. Halamajowa's house and everything inside it. They have even sent tax officials to assess the value of her property. In the course of their inspection, the Russians discover the hayloft in which we were hidden—including the fleas in the straw, which have survived and bite them savagely. They also find the buckets with traces of our slop still visible in them. Among the items confiscated by the Soviets are Mrs. Halamajowa's pigs and chickens that helped conceal our presence in the hayloft.

• • •

Later we learn how Mrs. Halamajowa made the trip to Lanzut and what she found there. We get the details from a friend of ours who met her on the way.

After crossing the border into the Polish Republic and traveling on foot for some time, Mrs. Halamajowa reached the town of Yaroslaw. Hungry and exhausted from the midsummer heat, she sat down on a curb near the town hall to rest. A friend of mine, Pinchas Stelzer, one of the few Jews who survived in Yaroslaw, happened to pass by. Seeing an elderly woman sitting dejectedly on the curb with her handbag and satchel beside her, he stopped to ask her whether he could do anything for her and where she had come from. When Mrs. Halamajowa replied that she had come from Sokal, Pinchas asked her, "Do you know whether there are any Jews left there?" She answered, "Yes, a few." He asked her whether she knew the Maltz family and whether any of them had survived. At the mention of our name, Mrs. Halamajowa seemed to forget that she was desperately tired. She straightened up and her eyes shone as she told Pinchas about us. Pinchas took her to his home, where his wife gave her a good meal and insisted that she spend the night with them before continuing on her journey.

When Mrs. Halamajowa arrived at Lanzut, her daughter Hela had tragic news to tell her. Her son, who had done so much to help her provide for our needs in the hayloft, had been murdered by the Germans as a "security risk." Mrs. Halamajowa went to the village where he had been executed to find out where he was buried so that she could have a tombstone put up in his memory. But no one whom she questioned seemed to know where the Germans had disposed of her son's body.

• • •

It is harvest time now in Sokal. The fields our family owned on the outskirts of town were farmed by Ukrainians. I go to the Soviet authorities, explaining to them that I am the rightful owner of the fields and requesting permission to reap the crops the Ukrainians planted there. The Soviets refuse my request; they claim that the land is now the property of the Soviet state and that I therefore have no right to it. I argue that I have the right to harvest the grain that was grown on my land. Finally, the Soviets propose a compromise. They will permit me to harvest 40 percent of this year's crop. But now that I have won my point I realize that it would not be safe for me, or any member of my family, to be seen harvesting these fields. The Ukrainians might shoot us. So I don't claim my harvest.

• • •

Five Jews from Sokal have been drafted into the Red Army. The Russians have assured us that Jewish draftees will only be assigned to labor service behind the lines. They will not be sent to the front because it is understood that capture by the Germans would mean torture, if not instant death, for a Jewish soldier from Poland.

Sokal, late August, 1944

The Soviets have not kept their promise about the Jewish draftees. They are lumping the Jews with the Ukrainians whom they consider traitors and whom they immediately send to the battle lines. The five Jews from Sokal were sent to the fighting front; three of them have been killed and two seriously wounded.

• • •

We have reports that a few Jews have returned to Lvov. Others have moved there from the surrounding countryside. Perhaps a fairly large Jewish community will rise there upon the ruins of the old. For a while I thought that my family should think of leaving Sokal and settling in Lvov also.

But life in Sokal is beginning to look almost normal. A few Ukrainians who fled from the Russians have returned, and some Poles from West Galicia have also settled there. The Russians are organizing state-operated stores to generate jobs. Our women are doing a little "unofficial" business on the black market. One way or the other, the people in Sokal are making a living, and that includes us Jews. I have a job as a buyer with a state-operated agricultural produce cooperative. So I decide that, at least for the present, we should stay in Sokal.

• • •

The handful of Jews—about 30 in all—who have returned to Sokal stick together like one large family.* The Gentiles don't seem to mind that we are back. Almost every German tells stories about having given food or other help to Jews during the German occupation. If you believe them, it was never they, but only the others, who helped strip the bodies of dead Jews and pull the gold teeth from their mouths after an Aktion.

The real picture is different. One neighbor tells me about a Ukrainian who agreed to give shelter to a Jew, then killed him and buried him in his garden. One foreman made it a practice to break into bunkers, pull out Jewish girls by their hair and turn them over to the Gestapo.

There is a cobbler in town who is doing very well now that the Russians are here. He has been appointed manager of a shoe manufacturing cooperative and his son has a job at the post office. During the German occupation, father and son regularly appeared at the town square to select Jews for work at their cobblery shop. They knew of one Jewish cobbler who failed to report at the town square for assignment to a labor detail. So the Gentile cobbler went to the Jewish cobbler's home, seized him and dragged him into the town square. There, the Germans ordered the Jewish cobbler to perform various humiliating exercises and took pictures of him while he did them. I hear such stories almost every day.

I report all these stories to the Soviet authorities, but they tell me they cannot do very much at present because Russia and Germany are still at war. Once the war has officially ended, the Russians will have the murderers tried and executed.

---

* This number does not include the few Jews from other localities who came to Sokal after the war.

Sokal, September, 1944

The High Holidays are coming. Rosh HaShanah will be on September 18 and 19; Yom Kippur, on September 27. I request permission from the Soviet authorities to open one of our synagogues for services. Permission is granted. Gentiles bring us prayer books they discovered in various places, and even a *shofar* (ram's horn). Of course, they expect to be compensated for their cooperation, and we gladly pay. We clear away the broken glass and other debris from inside the synagogue.

We decide not to use the synagogue for evening services on Rosh HaShanah, but only in the daytime, because people are afraid to walk through the street of the Synagogues after dark.

Each person brings his own little chair and a small table (for use as a reading stand) from home because only the bare walls of the synagogue are left. The women's balcony is neither fit nor safe for use; besides, our congregation is tiny. So the women sit on the main floor, separate from the men, but with no partition between them.

We have several men left who can take part in conducting the services. We even have two *kohanim*, descendants of the High Priest Aaron, brother of Moses, to chant the Priestly Blessing at the festival services: Dr. Kindler and his older son. (Eli, the younger son, has not yet reached the age of 13 when he will become eligible to assume a function at synagogue services.)

• • •

Since Rosh HaShanah services went smoothly without trouble, we decide to use the synagogue not only for the services on Yom Kippur itself, but also for the solemn *Kol Nidrei* service on Yom Kippur Eve. Again, no trouble. But afterwards we realize that we were very lucky. We could have been attacked and even murdered. Just three dozen Jews gathered in one room are a tempting target. So we decide to hold Sukkoth services (October 2 and 3 and again on October 9 and 10 this year) not at the synagogue but at my home.

• • •

After Yom Kippur I go to Lvov to obtain a safe-conduct pass. To get from Sokal to Lvov (both cities are occupied by the Soviets), you have to pass through a "Polish corridor," an area that is now part of the newly-established Republic of Poland. I travel in a Russian military car until the border between Soviet-occupied territory and the Polish corridor.

Inside what is now Poland, I stop another military truck. We pass through the town of Dobroczyn. The streets have been plowed up. There are wrecked tanks and remains of military vehicles everywhere; not a trace of the many factories that were here before the war. The mills have been burned down and the railroad station is in ruins. Only a few houses in the old Jewish neighborhood are still there. But not a trace is left of the synagogue or the *Beth Medrash*. Armed Polish militiamen, accompanied by Russian soldiers are patrolling the streets.

In Novodorsk and Klissow people are walking through the streets with a dazed, vacant look on their faces as is they were still in a state of shock.

Back inside Soviet territory, we pass through the town of Most. Not a sign of Jewish life there; only ruins. Driving through Zolkiew, where my wife's family used to live before the war, I note that the historic old synagogue building is still standing, but there is no glass in the windows. It makes me think of the empty eyesockets of a blind man.

Lvov, October, 1944

When you see Lvov, you can tell that this city has passed through a devastating war. There is no public transportation. The streets that once bustled with Jews are deserted. I report to the Jewish Committee, which has set up headquarters in the city's one surviving Jewish schoolhouse. I meet Jews from surrounding towns and villages who want to settle in Lvov.

The Jewish Committee has set up a register of all Jews presently in Lvov, so that anyone wishing to know whether relatives or friends have survived here, or have turned up here since the liberation, can go to the Committee office and look through the register of names.

I remain here in Lvov for the last days of the Sukkoth (Tabernacles) festival. On the Eighth Day (October 9 this year), I go to the synagogue and recite *Yizkor*, the memorial prayer for the dead. This is the first time in my life that I am in the synagogue during *Yizkor*. Before the war, when both my parents were still living, I would go outside at this point, returning to the synagogue when the *Yizkor* prayer had been completed. It was a time-honored custom for people whose parents were still alive not to be inside the synagogue during the prayer for the dead.* But now I have lost not only my father but also my daughter Lifshe and my sister Chaye Dvora, and so my place is in the synagogue with all the other mourners.

The synagogue is packed. It seems that almost every Jew in Lvov has come to recite the *Yizkor* prayer. The sermon before *Yizkor* is delivered by a Rabbi Steinberg of Brody; I am told he is the only known surviving rabbi in all of Galicia.** This is the first time in five years that I have heard Yiddish spoken before a public gathering. At times the sobbing in the congregation becomes so loud that the rabbi has to stop and wait for a little quiet.

This congregation is a mix of many kinds of survivors. Some have completely lost touch with their Judaism. A number of women are living with Gentile men who saved their lives during the Nazi occupation. I also see a few Russian army officers. They have come to the synagogue, I think, not so much to celebrate the Sukkoth festival as to join in mourning their dead.

Whoever knows the past of the great Jewish community of Lemberg, as Lvov used to be known, is heartsick to see the sad handful that has remained of all the many, many Jews who once lived, worked and prayed here. A side room of the synagogue is filled with Torah scrolls that were buried in the ground to hide them from the Germans and have just been dug out. There are altogether 500 of these scrolls, still damp and smelling of the wet soil. I am told that virtually every Jew who comes to Lvov—and that includes Russian army officers—makes a point of going to see the remnants of these sacred scrolls.

Sokal, late October, 1944

Back in Sokal, I find two new arrivals who spent the Nazi years

---

* Unlike the Mourner's Kaddish, which is purely a praise and sanctification of God's name and contains no mention of death or mourning, *Yizkor* specifically honors the memory of close relatives, notably parents, with each mourner silently uttering the names of his or her dead. *Yizkor* (May God remember. . . ."), which is recited on the major Jewish holidays, assumed special poignancy during the years immediately following the Holocaust when synagogues were filled with worshippers mourning the recent loss of their entire families.

** Rabbi Steinberg later settled in the United States, on New York's West Side, where he remained until his death. He left no children.

hiding in the woods. One is Reuben Lanes, a distant relative of mine; the other is Leibush Schiffenbauer's brother Aaron. I have taken Reuben Lanes into my home, stripped him of his rags, and given him new clothes. Along with 40 other Jews, Reuben and his family escaped from the ghetto of their native village and fled to the woods. The Laneses are the only survivors of the group; the other 40 were murdered by the Ukrainians.

Reuben Lanes and Aaron Schiffenbauer say they know the location of the mass grave where these 40 dead are buried. They should be exhumed and given a proper burial in a Jewish cemetery. But although this mass grave is only about eight kilometers from Sokal, we don't dare to visit it because we know that any Jew who shows his face in that area may be a target for a trigger-happy Ukrainian.

Lanes and Schiffenbauer, in their primitive bunker in the woods, didn't even know when the Germans left. They had already prepared to spend the coming winter in the woods. They went out at night to forage nearby fields for potatoes, beets and cabbage. There was only one problem: they had no matches to light fires for heat and cooking. During the summer they made fires by catching sunlight through a piece of glass, but in the winter there would not be enough sunlight for that. So, one evening after dark, they paid a call to an old Gentile woman they knew in a neighboring village and asked her whether she could give them a box of matches. The woman said she was sorry she couldn't help them. When the Germans had been there, she could always get plenty of matches but now that the Bolsheviks had come, there were no more matches to be had for love or money. That's how Lanes and Schiffenbauer first learned that the Germans had gone. But since they couldn't be sure they could trust the woman, or that she really knew, they went back into the woods. The next night they ventured out again, this time to another village, and asked a Gentile man whether it was true that the Russians had come. He informed them that the Russians had already been there for three months. So the next morning Lanes and Schiffenbauer left their bunkers and went to Lvov. From there, they came to Sokal.

A boy from Sokal has returned from Russia. He was drafted into the Red Army back in 1939 when the Russians received part of Sokal under the Molotov-Ribbentrop agreement. He was in the Red Army for four years and was wounded three times. His name is Hertz Mehl; he holds the rank of sergeant and has returned to Sokal to find out whether any members of his family have survived. He hasn't found anyone. I have taken him into my home for a little rest and recuperation.

• • •

I have been acting as the unofficial mailman for the Jews of Sokal and Zolkiew. I go to the post offices of both places to collect all mail addressed to Jews and distribute it because the local mailmen simply don't feel like doing it. In some cases, when I can't locate the addressee, I open the letters and answer them myself.

That is how I have made contact, for instance, with several other Jewish boys from Sokal who, like Hertz Mehl, were drafted into the Red Army in 1939. A letter from one boy, Itzik Dachs, a non-commissioned officer in the Red Army, was addressed to "Any Jew Who Has Survived." I had to write to him that his whole family is gone. He wrote in reply, "Tell the murderers that I will return and make them pay for killing my family."

• • •

A little post-liberation geography: The River Bug is not the natural boundary between the newly-established independent Polish Republic and the territory annexed by the Soviet Union. The area on the west bank of the river, which includes part of Sokal (and its railroad station), as well as the towns of Belz, Krystynopol and Warisz, now belongs to the Hrubieszow district of the Polish Republic.

The east bank of the river, including our homes and the main section of Sokal, has been taken over by the Ukrainian Soviet Socialist Republic, whose capital is the city of Kiev.

• • •

Sokal's main street is lined with the graves of Soviet soldiers who fell in the battle for Sokal. The monuments bear inscriptions and, in some cases, photographs of the fallen soldier. Several names sound Jewish.

In the park, opposite the new governor's residence, are graves of Soviet officials who were captured by the Germans in 1941. The Germans took these prisoners into the Potosycze woods, shot them and buried them in a mass grave. Now the Russians have exhumed them and reinterred them in the park.

At the corner of the Tartakow highway, where the old governor's mansion used to be, and also at the new Soviet courthouse, there are large black billboards giving the total number of men, women and children killed, and the total number of buildings destroyed, "by the Fascist murderers" in Sokal. The grand total amounts to 12,000 people killed and several hundred buildings destroyed. We Jews know what the black billboards do not mention: that almost all the men, women and children killed "by the Fascist murderers" in Sokal were Jewish and virtually all the buildings that were destroyed were once owned by Jews.

Most of the Gentiles now living in Sokal are Ukrainian; only a handful of Poles, most of them old and destitute, have remained. On Sundays these Poles celebrate mass among the ruins of the Polish Catholic church in the center of town. The service is conducted by the only Polish Catholic priest left in Sokal. Construction of that Catholic church began during the 1920s and was completed only in 1939. When the Germans came two years later, they reduced the church to rubble. On alternate Sundays the same priest celebrates mass at the church in the suburb of Babeniec.

The Ukrainian intelligentsia has fled from Sokal along with the retreating Germans. Many Ukrainians volunteered to serve in a special Ukrainian division of the SS. Among these volunteers were the sons of Sokal's Greek Orthodox bishop. So the bishop, afraid that the Russians will punish him because of his sons, has taken off for parts unknown. Hardly any worshippers attend mass at the Ukrainian Church of Sts. Peter and Paul nowadays. The icons in the church were riddled by German bullets in 1941. Yisroel Gross, a Jewish tinsmith, was ordered by the Germans to patch up the icons with bits of metal from bombed buildings (most of them owned by Jews).

Gentiles are selling bootleg alcohol in the marketplace. The local peasants use the alcohol to manufacture whiskey, for which the Russian soldiers are good customers.

There are still signs that many Jews once lived here, for instance, anti-Semitic graffiti on the walls and signs over storefronts warning Poles not to buy from Jews. Most of Sokal's present population can't read these signs because they are in Polish, not Ukrainian. But all the rivers of blood that have been washed from the cobbled streets of Sokal cannot erase the obscene Polish graffiti.

Russian border guards are stationed on our side of the River Bug over a span of 50 kilometers. They are billeted in the theological seminary, in the courthouse and in some private homes. Staff headquarters, complete with a Russian colonel and assorted officers of every rank, have been set up on the site where Zulchinsky, the cattle dealer and wholesale butcher used to have his place of business. The headquarters building is surrounded by barbed wire fences. The entrance is heavily guarded and civilians are admitted only by special permit.

Sokal, November, 1944

The Ukrainians in our area are not on good terms with the Soviet authorities. Most of the Bandera gangs, men and women, from the villages around Sokal are still hiding out in the woods, armed to the teeth, and hold up Soviet soldiers. The Soviets may be the rulers of the town, but the Bandera gangs reign supreme in the surrounding countryside, especially at night. When the Bandera gangs seize a Jew, they consider it a prize catch. The ordinary Ukrainians feel the same way. Everybody wants to get his hands on the victim because they all want to participate in the heroic act of killing a Jew. They literally slash Jews to pieces with their machetes.

Whenever I have business with a Ukrainian in town, I tell my family where I am going and when I expect to be back, because it sometimes happens that a Jew leaves his home to keep an appointment with a Ukrainian and is never seen again. Most of the time I avoid going on such errands by myself; I usually take another person with me. I stay home after dark because a Jew who is out at night can get a bullet in his back and no one will ever find out who did it. The door of my house is locked securely at all times. If someone knocks on the door, we ask who it is before we open. If we know the voice, we open; if not, we don't. I always carry a couple of guns with me so that I can defend myself.

The Russians, too, have their hands full with the Ukrainians and the Bandera types. Hardly a day passes without a Soviet official being killed. If the Russians discover one of their dead, they bury him with full honors, including the Communist clenched-fist salute, as a victim of the "Fascist murderers." The speakers at the funeral extol the merits of their fallen comrade and vow at his open grave that they will avenge his death.

The Soviets really don't allow murders of their own men to go unavenged. Their soldiers and border guards are waging constant battle against the Bandera gangs. The wooded areas outside Sokal are surrounded by Russian soldiers in full battle gear; sometimes the shooting continues for days until all the Ukrainians have been flushed out from the woods.

Every day new Ukrainian prisoners taken in the villages are brought into Sokal—men and women, their hands tied behind their backs with thick ropes. The block of prison cells at Soviet staff head-quarters is always filled to capacity with Ukrainian prisoners. They are herded together so closely that there is virtually no space between them. The men are locked up separately from the women. The prison diet consists of a bowl of watery soup and a piece of sawdust bread twice each day. After the trial, those found guilty of minor offences are sent straight to prison from the battlefront. (After all, there's still a war going on against the Germans.) Those declared guilty of more serious offenses are sent to labor camps deep inside Russia, from where they are not likely to return. Those convicted of a major crime are dispatched to the next world on the spot without the need for prisons or labor camps. Their families who lived with them are shipped off to Siberia and their possessions are confiscated by the Soviet State.

• • •

The Russian army officer in charge of local operations against the Bandera gangs is Jewish. He often comes to see me and I tip him off on the whereabouts of big-time Ukrainian murderers who are known to me. The Jews from the neighboring villages also report Nazi collaborators who are still at large. The officer enters the villages with his men, tracks down the murderers and finishes them off.

• • •

The Soviet authorities in Sokal are on good terms with us, because they regard Jews as true friends. Some Soviet army officers even accept invitations from Jews for a drink or a meal. But we are careful to associate only with the true-blood Soviet Russians. We avoid officers of Ukrainian background because they are just as rabidly anti-Semitic as the ordinary Ukrainian civilian.

• • •

The handful of Jewish children in Sokal are enrolled in Ukrainian schools. Since the old schoolhouse was blown up by the retreating Germans, all the classes meet in the building of the high school. There is at least one Jewish student in each class. The superintendent of public instruction in Sokal is none other than the son-in-law of Mrs. Metritzky, the former neighbor of our own Mrs. Halamajowa.

Once every few months the parents meet at the Sokal Athletic

Clubhouse to hear reports about their children's scholastic progress. The Ukrainians are whispering among themselves that the Jewish students are being given special privileges at school. The truth is that the Jewish pupils happen to be the best students.

Meanwhile, the older Ukrainian students, many of whom helped celebrate the *Aktionen* in Sokal with parades and anti-Semitic songs, are studying military science at school. Their teacher is a Jew by the name of Schreibman, who served in the Red Army and lost an eye in the war. His assistant is none other than Sergeant Hertz Mehl, who has been officially transferred to Sokal and is still living at my home.

• • •

Movies are shown every Saturday and Sunday at the Sokolny Theater. My wife and I never go because we can't bear to enter the theater which was always filled with Jewish children in the olden days. But our little Chaim, who is now eight years old, goes there with his Ukrainian friends from school. Whenever he is late coming home from the movies, Chana and I get worried and rush to the theater to look for him. I touch the shoulder of a grownup in the last row and ask him whether he has seen my son Chaim. Everyone in town knows Chaim. He seems to be the only little boy by that name in all of Sokal.

• • •

Mrs. Metritzky and her son Romek visit us often. In fact, we've become quite friendly. She comes to me whenever she needs help or advice. One day a Soviet major from staff headquarters (people say he's Jewish, too), visited the Metritzky home. When he saw the elegant furniture there, he insisted that it must have been stolen from a Jewish home. So he had some of the furniture removed from the house and took it for himself. Mrs. Metritzky went to court with witnesses to testify that the furniture was her own, and had not been stolen from Jews. She won her case, but the major refused to return the furniture to her. She appealed her case at the district court in Lvov and won again, but the major still would not give her the furniture. She asked me what she should do. She was afraid that if she appealed her case further, she might be sent to Siberia.

But she thinks she has found a way of making sure the Russians won't attempt to confiscate her remaining furniture. She has taken a Russian lodger into her home: Schreibman, her son Romek's military science teacher.

• • •

I have made another trip to Lvov. There is talk that a Polish government, whose seat is in Lublin (the capital, Warsaw, is still in German hands), is about to sign a repatriation agreement with the Ukrainian Soviet Socialist Republic. Under this agreement, I hear, all Ukrainians living in the Polish Republic will be given the opportunity to resettle in the Soviet Union, while Poles—Gentiles and Jews—now living in Soviet-occupied territory will be repatriated to Poland, if they wish. Poles interested in repatriation will be released from their jobs by the Soviet authorities and permitted to leave without difficulty. They will be allowed to take with them movable property, not in excess of half a ton in weight. Farmers will be allowed to also take their cattle and other farm animals, with the Soviet government footing the bill for their transportation. The value of the homes the Polish repatriates leave behind in Soviet territory, will be appraised by the Soviet authorities, and when their former owners arrive in Poland, they will be given homes there with approximately the same assessed value.

I go to the headquarters of the Jewish Committee in Lvov to talk to people and learn how they feel about this opportunity. The Polish Jews to whom I talk in Lvov seem to like the idea. A repatriation commission is already working in Lvov, registering people seeking repatriation to Poland. Most of those who have registered thus far, I am told, are Jews. The Gentile Poles don't want to leave their homes. They consider that, as far as they are concerned, Lvov is Poland, no matter who is in charge.

When I ask a university professor, a Gentile, whether he will request repatriation to the new Polish Republic, he indignantly replies, "Most certainly not. We Poles will never leave Lvov. Never mind that Lvov is occupied by the Russians now. Lvov has been a Polish city from time immemorial. The graves in our ancient cemetery attest to that. Think of the great Polish kings and poets who are buried here! Besides, England has guaranteed the restoration of Poland's borders as they were in 1939, before the war. It was part of Poland then, and mark my words, when this war is over, the Soviets will have to give Lvov back to the Polish Republic.

• • •

Back in Sokal, the Jews are in a dither. We hear that a repatriation commission is due to arrive in Sokal soon to register Polish repatriates. The Jews of Sokal have called a meeting under the chairmanship of Dr. Kindler to decide what their attitude should be. Some say they are afraid to register because the offer may be a Russian trap; if they ask for repatriation to Poland, the Soviets may arrest them as traitors. Others again see resettlement in Poland as their only chance for freedom when this war is over. They argue that if they don't seize this opportunity to leave Soviet territory and move to the Polish Republic, they will be cut off from the world outside forever. They will never be able to see their relatives who survived the war in other countries, much less go to the one place where they feel that Jews will truly have a chance to rebuild their lives: *Eretz Yisrael.*

The discussion ends in the general concensus that Jews of Polish origin should register for repatriation to Poland.

• • •

The repatriation commission had begun to work in Sokal. I report to the commission, turn in my Soviet identification papers and receive a repatriation permit. The document instantly transforms my family and me into what we were before Hitler came: citizens of the Polish Republic.

I give notice to the agricultural produce cooperative for which I have been working. My boss is surprised. "Why should a Jew want to live under the Poles, with those Polack anti-Semites? Aren't you afraid of pogroms?"

It is strange that this man should ask me such a question. Judging from his last name, and the slight accent with which he speaks Russian, he may be a Pole himself. I tell him very candidly that I have no intention of living in Poland permanently. What my family and I really want to do is leave the blood-drenched soil of Europe behind us and go to Palestine. We want to stay in Poland only until the war is over and everyone will be free to travel wherever he wants to go.

• • •

The Soviet authorities in Sokal don't seem happy that so many Jews want to leave. They are offering Jews the best jobs to induce them to stay in Sokal. It is clear that the Ukrainians, on the other hand, can hardly wait to be rid of this little handful of Jews so that they will be free to wear the clothes they have stolen from the Jews without some Jewish survivor stopping them in the street and asking them where they got the clothes. One Jewish girl recognized a garment of hers on a Ukrainian woman and tore it right off the woman's body, in the middle of the street.

• • •

There have been incidents between Jews and Ukrainians in the marketplace. It's been a long time since the Ukrainians have seen Jews there. One day I come upon a crowd of Ukrainians pushing and shoving each other in front of a stall. A woman yells, "Push, push, push! Just like the Jews used to do!" I march straight up to her and say to her, "Don't you dare talk that way about the Jews ever again! Your people have spilled enough Jewish blood already!" She is frightened and shuts up. Another time a Jewish woman buys a live chicken from a peasant woman in the marketplace. "Can't you sell your chickens to anybody else but Jews?" a man asks her afterward. Aaron Schiffenbauer, who happens to be standing nearby, calls over an NKVD man. The Gentile is placed under arrest and sentenced to two weeks in prison.

January, 1945

We're still here in Sokal back at my old job. Winter isn't a good time for moving. More important, parts of Poland are still occupied by the Germans. We plan to wait until the spring.

• • •

We've had our first Jewish wedding here since the war. The bridegroom was a young partisan fighter from Zolkiew, who came to Sokal with his fiancée. We all helped prepare the wedding, including the cooking and baking. Virtually all the Jews in town attended the ceremony, which was performed by Mendel Igel, who had had rabbinic training. Among the guests were the Soviet prosecutor and his wife. The postmaster came, too, and played some songs on his guitar. The festivities lasted until midnight.

• • •

The Ukrainians in Sokal are becoming increasingly restive under the Soviets. As a result, the Soviet authorities have imposed harsh restrictions on them. This has put a strain on life in Sokal. People can now leave town only with special permission; the limits of Sokal are heavily guarded. If you have to travel to Lvov, the nearest big city, on business, you can no longer take the direct route, which is through the "Polish corridor." You must take the circuitous routes, through woods and other unsafe terrain, until you get to a railroad station from which you can take a train to Lvov. Most people make the trip in convoys of cars and trucks. Especially a Jew who attempts to take the trip by himself, does so at the risk of his life.

Sokal, late February 1945

I am spending most of my time tracking down Nazis and Nazi collaborators and reporting them to Soviet staff headquarters. The Soviets assure me that all these murderers will be brought to justice when the war is over.

• • •

So far we haven't been able to carry out our plan to build fences around the mass graves and around the Jewish cemetery, or to exhume the bodies of Jews for reinterrment in the Jewish cemetery, for the simple reason that it dangerous for Jews to show their faces on the outskirts of town where the mass graves are located.

February 27: Purim, the first Purim after the liberation of Sokal. We all gather at Dr. Kindler's place for a little party.* Among the guests are several officers from Soviet staff headquarters who are Jewish.

Sokal, March, 1945

My family and I, and most of the other Jewish survivors, are ready to leave Sokal. Before we go, we bid farewell to the only witnesses that will be left, once we are gone, to testify before history that Jews once lived in this town. Along with a group of others who will be "repatriated" to Poland, my family and I visit the graves in the old Jewish cemetery. It is difficult to identify the ancient graves. Only a few headstones are still standing. We find headstones of more recent origin, marking the graves of relatives and friends who died before the war, and we pay them a tribute of silent tears.

At some distance, out in the fields, I see two figures moving. They are carrying guns but don't look like soldiers. Are they Bandera men? We are ready to run. But then somebody says, "Those aren't Ukrainians! They're NKVD men!" Relieved, we linger in the cemetery a little longer.

It is strange. In all the years of the Nazi terror I never had shed a tear, not even when my father was taken away and when my wife told

---

* The merry holiday of Purim, which comes a month before Passover, celebrates the deliverance of Persia's Jewish community from the evil plot of Haman, prime minister of King Ahasuerus, to kill all the Jews in the Persian Empire. This event is the subject of the Book of Esther.

me that we had lost our child, Lifshe. Now that my family and I are about to start our journey to freedom, I seem to be crying all the time. . . .

On March 15, the first transport of Jewish repatriates leaves Sokal for Poland. They will travel to Zabusche, near the River Bug, where they will have to wait several days for a westbound Soviet troop train.

• • •

On March 19, 1945, we remove our sister Chaye Dvora from her grave under Mrs. Halamajowa's apple tree to give her a Jewish funeral in the Jewish cemetery. Shmelke and I, assisted by a few other men, spend hours digging for our sister's remains, but can't find them The next day I ask a Ukrainian acquaintance to help us. This was a man I could trust; he worked in our family business for 20 years and he cried with joy when he heard we had survived.

With this man's help, we finally locate the remains of our Chaye Dvora. We place them on a wagon, and virtually all the Jews still left in Sokal walk behind it to escort our sister to her final resting place. This is probably the last Jewish funeral that will ever be held in Sokal.

Schmelke and Chaim after liberation from the hayloft, 1946.

I make the following entry, in Hebrew, into a blank page of my prayer book: "On the second day of the week (Monday), the fifth day of the month of Nisan, 5705, we gave a Jewish burial to our sister Chaye Dvora, peace be upon her soul. Her grave is located about five meters from the monument of Eliahu Zev Strauss."

• • •

After our sister's funeral, we start preparations for Passover, which will begin on March 29 this year. The first *seder* will be held on Wednesday evening, March 28. First of all, we need matzoth. I buy pure wheat from a Ukrainian on Switezow Street. We grind the wheat with a primitive mill operated by horsepower. The millstone is a headstone the Ukrainians uprooted from one of the old graves in the Jewish cemetery. I can still see the lettering of the Hebrew epitaph. Later we learn that virtually all the millstones in Sokal are headstones from Jewish graves.

April, 1945

Passover, the festival of freedom, has come. We are celebrating our first Passover after liberation. But what freedom do we actually have here in Sokal? We are not free to visit or travel where we please. It is a freedom tinged with grief for the past and apprehension about the future. Especially on this holiday, we feel the true measure of our pain and sorrow.

Dr. Kindler has decided to leave Sokal with his family, but just now there is no way of obtaining transportation, so neither he nor anyone else can leave at the moment. Kindler has contacted a Polish officer he knows, a Jewish fellow, stationed in Zamosc, who has promised to send a truck to take them to Zamosc, where he will meet them. From there he will help them start on the next phase of their journey.

• • •

The River Bug has overflowed its banks and the one temporary bridge that was built after the liberation and that linked us with Poland, has been washed away. But Kindler and his family have left just the same. They and their baggage were ferried across the river. Kindler's Polish friend will meet them there and drive them the remaining 120 kilometers to Zamosc, where they will wait for a train traveling in the direction of Lublin.

• • •

There is hardly anyone left here for me to talk with. Even the few Jews who insisted until recently they would stay in Sokal, are now thinking seriously about leaving.

Dr. Macziewicz, still the only doctor in town, and Mrs. Halamajowa's former neighbor, Mrs. Metritzky, are trying to talk me into staying here. "Why on earth would you want to go to Poland?" they ask me. "Don't you know that Poland's a slaughterhouse for Jews?"

[*At the time we don't believe what these Ukrainians are saying. We think they are saying it only because they hate the Poles. Only later will we see that they were right. After the war, many Poles felt called upon to finish the job Hitler had begun. On July 4, 1946, there was a pogrom in the town of Kielce.*]

• • •

We spend virtually all our time thinking of ways to leave Sokal for Poland as soon as possible. There are two routes open to us. One is to travel by car or wagon (Ukrainian Sokal still has no railroad station) to Lvov, where we can wait for a train that will take us across the Polish border. The other alternative is to travel to the border station, Zabusch, and hitch a ride on a truck returning to Hrubieszow after picking up cattle and grain. However, this route is risky for Jews. On the other hand, it's dangerous for Jews to travel to Lvov at all.

I have an idea: I'll buy myself a wagon with two horses. I'll put on a Ukrainian peasant costume, get Ukrainian identification papers and take my family out of Sokal in the wagon, in several shifts.

No one must know that we're leaving. We don't want the Bandera gangsters on our trail.

When I tell my son Chaim that we're leaving Sokal and going to Poland, he says he's not going. He doesn't want to leave his Ukrainian school, his Ukrainian teachers and his Ukrainian friends.

• • •

My plan to go to Poland by way of Lvov has fallen through. So I sell the horse and wagon I have bought and choose the Hrubieszow route. I intend to go to Hrubieszow by truck I will hire, with Chana, my mother, my sister Yitte and Chaim. From Hrubieszow we will proceed to the railroad station in Zamosc and take a train to Cracow, where we will meet Shmelke, Leah and Feyge Chashe, who have already left Sokal. I have set the date and time for our departure: Wednesday, May 9, 1945, at four o'clock in the morning, when it's still dark and we are not likely to meet anyone.

May 8–9, 1945

The night before our departure, I am awakened from my sleep by heavy artillery fire. I look out the window and see fires on the Tartakow highway. Is this the full-scale Bandera gang attack on Sokal everybody has been expecting?

We now have a radio. I turn it on, and soon I know the reason for the shooting. Germany has surrendered! The artillery fire is a salute to the Allied victory!

We get out of bed—Chana, my mother and Yitte—and are ready to leave. But where is Chaim? He's not in his bed. Everybody goes off in another direction looking for him. Where could he have gone? Finally we discover him at the house of his best friend, a Ukrainian boy. We have a lot of trouble persuading him to come with us, but in the end he gives in.

And so, on the day following the end of this accursed war, we leave Sokal behind. We cross the border at Zabusch and arrive in Hrubieszow. We have entered Poland, the first stop on our journey to freedom.

צַר לִי עָלֶיךָ אָחִי יְהוֹנָתָן, נָעַמְתָּ לִי מְאֹד (שמואל ב')

"I grieve for you, my brother Jonathan, I loved you so."

(Second Samuel)

by Shmelke Maltz

These are the words of King David, rest his soul, concerning Jonathan. With these words I express the sudden loss of my brother, Moshe, son of our martyred father, Joseph. Great is the pain our family feels by your departure, recalling the dark, Job-like days you endured in the hospital, as we kept you company, I, Yetta, your sons, as you turned to me with that constant question: Shmelke, could you possibly explain to me why we, of all people, survived, a handful out of an entire city? This question was always on his mind, even in those last days, when he was no longer the same Moshe.

My answer to him was that this was the will of the Creator, but at the same time I thought to myself, perhaps this was also the reward for honoring father and mother, as the Holy Torah assures us by saying, "Honor your father and mother, that you may live long."

Yes, my brother, Moshe, when our mother, may the Holy One avenge her blood, was lying sick in the ghetto with that killing disease, typhus, and was having other kinds of trouble, with no help from the ghetto, only more seriously ill people lying in the same house with no food or water, dying like flies, one by one. The doctor said to me, Shmelke, could you bring some medicine from outside the ghetto, from the new apothecary? That meant certain death. But the writer of these lines did not waste any time thinking. He takes off his arm band with the Star of David and climbs the ghetto fence, risking his life, virtually committing martyrdom, and brings medicine for his sainted mother. And, behold, the medicine helps! The sainted woman would not taste anything that was not kosher. And we did the same for our father, and our unfortunate brother, in the horrible ghetto. With the help of the Almighty we observed the words of the prophet Isaiah, "Share your bread with the hungry, and do not ignore your flesh and blood."

And so I tried to answer my brother's question. Yes, Moshe, the prophet Ezekiel says in Chapter 14 that three *Tzadikim* endured terrible times—Noah, Daniel and Job. Noah lived through three worlds—he lived before, during and after the flood. You, my brother Moshe, also lived through three worlds, the world before the destruction, which was a world of great men, of great yeshivot, of vibrant Jewish life with many *Tzadikim*, great scholars, merchants, intellectuals and experts in every field. This was the first era. The second era was the time when the world was burning, especially the Jewish world, when the German murderers with the Ukrainian and other helpers, may their names perish, actualized the words, "The sword is consuming outside, and there is death in the home." They put to death without mercy, utilizing strange and unusual methods, men, women and children, not sparing anyone. This was the second, dark era. But you were privileged to live in a third world, when our Holy Land was rebuilt and now we have our own army to protect us. And you lived to see the demise of Communism, which murdered many innocent Jews, and which, by its own falsehood, had to perish. This is an enormous privilege, and, most important, the resurrection of the dry bones, predicted in solemn words by the prophet Ezekiel. And you gave rise to a family and had great fulfillment, true *nachas* from your two sons, and you lived to see grandchildren and great-grandchildren raised in the spirit of Judaism, prominent members of the community, generous people who do all they can to fulfill the commandment of charity and mercy.

May your soul be bound up in the bonds of eternal life!

ת.נ.צ.ב.ה.

Epilogue

Nearly two generations have gone by since Moshe (Morris) Maltz first recorded his Holocaust diary in Yiddish.

Years of Horror—Glimpse of Hope is an epic of survival written by a family man in the prime of his life, a son, a husband, father, brother and uncle who kept his own spirits high and applied his innate talent for leadership, his common sense and his wit (and even humor) to the day-to-day business of keeping his loved ones alive in an atmosphere of never-ending danger and apprehension.

Moshe Maltz's account stops with an entry for May 9, 1945, the day following the German surrender to the Allies. The rest of the Maltz story, which spans almost five decades after VE-Day and which still continues, was never committed to writing. But in order to be complete for the present generation, the Holocaust diary of Moshe Maltz must be followed by a final chapter. We want to know how the subsequent lives of the Maltz family were shaped by the Holocaust and by the sheer miracle of their survival. Hence this final chapter, which was put together with the unfailing cooperation of the generation of Maltzes that still recalls the days in the ghetto of Sokal and in Mrs. Halamajowa's hayloft.

Even as members of the Maltz family who survived emerged from their hiding place together, so, spurred on by Moshe Maltz's irrepressible optimism and enthusiasm for life, they also made their plans for the future together, as a family.

It was as a family, too, that the Maltzes, after the war, decided to resume the observances of Orthodox Judaism in which they had been raised. Like countless other Jews under the Nazi heel, the Maltzes had been compelled to transgress basic religious laws in order to remain alive.

• • •

On May 9, 1945, Moshe Maltz, his mother Rivkah and his sister Yitte left their home town, Sokal, on the first stage of their journey to freedom. Moshe's plan was that they should cross the Russian border

(Left to right) Nathan, Chana, Moshe and Chaim—Summer, 1957.

by truck into Poland in the dark before dawn. The first stop would be the town of Hrubieszow. From Hrubieszow they would again proceed, again by truck, to the nearest operating railroad station, in the town of Zamosc, where they would again take a train for Cracow. In Cracow they would join Moshe's wife Chana, their young son, Chaim, Moshe's sister Leah Letzter and Leah's little daughter Feyge Chashe, who had already crossed into Poland by another route.

From Cracow the family—eight in all—would go together to Czechoslovakia or Hungary, from where they would make their way into the American-occupied zone of Austria and seek shelter at a displaced persons' camp. In addition to their official function, which was to shelter homeless survivors of the Holocaust and refugees from Communist Eastern Europe, these "DP camps" were used as assembly centers by *B'richa* (literally: "Flight"), a daring, heroic and strictly illegal project launched by the Jewish underground of what was then the British Mandate of Palestine. In the teeth of British and Arab opposition, *B'richa* shepherded Holocaust survivors across the unstable borders of postwar Europe in flight from a war-ravaged continent to *Eretz*

Moshe, Chana and Chaim, summer 1946—Ebelsberg, Austria.

Fayga Chashe, Nathan and Chaim, fall, 1947—Ebelsberg, Austria.

Yisrael. There, in the Homeland of the Jewish people, they would be received with open arms, not as refugees with no other place to go, but as comrades in the task of rebuilding their land and, in the process, their own lives as well.

The Maltzes' journey began with a tragedy. The truck in which Moshe, Rivkah and Yitte Maltz traveled to Hrubieszow, skidded and turned over on the highway. Yitte was slightly hurt. Her mother Rivkah suffered more severe injuries. She was taken to the hospital in Hrubieszow, where she died on June 5, 1945. She was 64 years old.

Since the Jewish community of Hrubieszow had been wiped out by the Nazis, no one was there to help the Maltzes arrange their mother's funeral. They made a plain wooden box into which they placed Rivkah's body for burial in accordance with Orthodox Jewish tradition and bribed a Polish army officer to dig the grave in the old Jewish cemetery.

After observing *shiva,* the seven-day period of deep mourning, the Maltz family spent an additional week in Zamosc and then proceeded to Cracow. The seven remaining Maltzes—Moshe, Chana, Chaim, Yitte, Shmelke, Leah and Feyge Chashe—climbed aboard a Russian truck bound for Moravska Ostrava, a Czech city not far from the Polish border. From Moravska Ostrava they took a train for Budapest, arriving in the Hungarian capital just in time for the High Holidays. They attended Yom Kippur services at the famous Dohany ucca Synagogue (Tabaktempel), the largest and most impressive structure of its type in Europe.

The Maltzes and other Jewish refugees in Budapest received food and money from the American Jewish Joint Distribution Committee (JDC), which had set up an office in Budapest and which the Holocaust survivors, most of whom knew little or no English, fondly called "the Joint." Though, in view of "the Joint's" official status, this had to be strictly unofficial, "the Joint" had contacts also with representatives of *B'richa.* And so it was through "the Joint" that Moshe Maltz learned the date on which a *B'richa* refugee transport, escorted by Jewish underground veterans, would leave Budapest for the American zone of Austria.

Every phase of a *B'richa* journey had its own hardships and dangers. The British not only guarded the borders of *Eretz Yisrael* to keep out "illegal" immigrants, but also put pressure on Western governments and occupation authorities to be on the lookout for large groups of Jews moving in the general direction of the Mediterranean or Black Sea ports from which boats were likely to sail for Palestine. This meant that *B'richa* transports had to be kept small and had to cross from one country to another in border areas known to be deserted and unpatrolled. Frequently, this meant traveling under cover of darkness, on foot and by circuitous routes.

The seven Maltzes made the perilous journey from Hungary to Austria together, with Moshe's wife Chana carrying nine-year-old Chaim part of the way.

In the DP camps, refugees waited for their turn to join a *B'richa* transport, or for immigration papers sent by relatives from countries other than *Eretz Yisrael*—most often, the United States.

The Maltz family spent over three years in Austrian DP camps. From the late fall of 1945 until September 9, 1947, they were in Randshofen near Braunau am Inn. From there, they were transferred to Ebelsberg, where they remained until their departure for New York.

It was at the camp, virtually in the shadow of Braunau, birthplace of Adolf Hitler, that Chana Maltz gave birth to a second son, whom she and Moshe named Joseph Nathan. The arrival of this baby, on November 10, 1946, in a displaced persons' camp, bore eloquent witness to his parents' faith in the coming of better days. Moshe Maltz was then 44, and Chana, 37.

For a long time the Maltzes centered their hopes for the future on *Eretz Yisrael*. They eagerly awaited the formation of a *B'richa* transport that would have room for all of them to make the journey together from Randshofen to Haifa. But one day they received a letter from America, from Moshe's uncle, Sam Suchman, the uncle in Newark, New Jersey, to whom Moshe, back in Sokal, had written out a letter with the idea that his little daughter Lifshe should eventually send the letter to America if she, Lifshe, should be the sole member of the family to survive the war. Of course, that letter was gone, and so was Lifshe. . . . But now Sam Suchman wrote from Newark that he had happened to see, in the Sunday rotogravure section of *The Jewish Daily Forward*, a picture of life at the Randshofen camp and there, in the picture, he had identified Moshe, Chana, Yitte and Leah. He wrote that he had almost fainted from shock and joy. But where was his sister Rivkah?

Moshe and Schmelke in Israel—1981.

When Moshe wrote to Sam about Rivkah's death in the highway accident and the family's other losses during the war, Sam promptly replied that he wanted all of his sister's remaining family to come to live near him, in the United States.

The rest of the family agreed that since they wanted to remain together, Moshe Maltz made the decision that the family would accept the uncle's offer. And so Sam Suchman, in Newark, New Jersey, got started on the long, tortuous process of obtaining U.S. immigration papers for his two nephews, two nieces, one niece-in-law, two great-nephews and one great-niece.

While they were waiting in the camp for their American immigration visas to come through, Moshe Maltz and his brother Shmelke became active in the rich, varied Jewish cultural, religious and organizational life which the Jewish DP's developed when it became clear that months, if not years, might pass before they would be able to leave the camps for *Eretz Yisrael* or some other permanent home. Moshe and Shmelke organized a Randshofen branch of Mizrachi, the religious Zionist movement in which they both had been raised.

It was at Randshofen, too, that Shmelke performed an act of personal revenge. Quite by accident, he discovered Chernetsky, the Ukrainian mayor of Sokal who had been responsible for the shooting of at least 400 Jews, including Shmelke's brother-in-law, Eli Letzter. A number of Ukrainians, terrified of the Russians, had fled west and turned up in various DP camps in West Germany and Austria as refugees from Communism. Shmelke spotted one such Ukrainian on the main street of a village near Randshofen. Shmelke pointed him out to Moshe, who happened to be with him. "Are you an Ukrainian?" Shmelke asked the man. When the man said yes, Shmelke explained that he and his brother Moshe, too, were Ukrainians, from the town of Sokal. Shmelke then took the man to the village inn and bought him a good meal.

Before long, the Ukrainian had become sufficiently relaxed and talkative for Shmelke to proceed with the next step. "By the way," Shmelke began casually, "would you happen to know whatever became of that fellow whom the Germans appointed as mayor of Sokal back in 1941? Chernetsky—yes, I think that was his name." When the Ukrainian asked why Shmelke wanted to know, Shmelke explained that Chernetsky had been especially accommodating to him and that he, Shmelke, had not forgotten. In fact, he wanted to give Chernetsky a nice present. The Ukrainian thereupon told Shmelke that Chernetsky was now in a DP camp that had been set up for Polish refugees not far away, near Bad Ischl, once the favorite summer resort of Austria's emperor Francis Joseph I.

After the Ukrainian had left, Shmelke said to Moshe, "Now I know why I was chosen to survive the Nazi hell." Shmelke and Moshe then went to the office of the United Nations Relief and Rehabilitation Ad-

Charnetsky, former mayor of Sokal.

Sam (Schmelke) Maltz.

ministration, (UNRRA) at Randshofen and informed a staff member that they knew the whereabouts of a Ukrainian Nazi bigwig who had been personally involved in the massacre of 400 Jews in Sokal. The UNRRA man asked Shmelke whether he would be able to recognize Chernetsky in a lineup of soldiers from the Polish camp. When the uniformed men were paraded before him, Shmelke walked straight up to one of them. "Are you Chernetsky?" he asked. When the man replied that he was, Shmelke threw himself at him and started to belabor him with his bare fists and booted feet. Years later, in telling the story, Shmelke would say that he had felt the strength of six million Jews behind him, pushing him forward to avenge their murder. Probably satisfied that Chernetsky was only getting the punishment he deserved, the UNRRA official at first made no attempt to restrain Shmelke. But after about 15 minutes, apparently thinking that, for the sake of order, he could not permit Chernetsky to die without a proper court trial and sentence, the UNRRA man motioned to one of the soldiers to take Chernetsky away. Chernetsky was placed under arrest as a war criminal pending trial. He died three months later in an Allied military prison. Shmelke often wonders whether the beating he administered to Chernetsky contributed to his unexpected death.

On September 9, 1947, the Maltzes were among the displaced persons moved from Randshofen to Camp Ebelsberg. On December 28, 1948, the Maltz family—now consisting of five adults and three young children—left Ebelsberg to board the SS *Marine Flasher*, which set sail from Bremerhaven, Germany for America on January 7, 1949. Ten days later, on January 17, 1949, the boat, an old troopship set aside for transporting DPs to the United States, landed in Boston harbor, where the Maltzes were greeted by their uncle Sam Suchman. The family settled in Newark, New Jersey, where Sam owned a prosperous wholesale dairy products firm.

Originally, Moshe and Shmelke had planned to open a retail grocery store together in Newark. But when it was pointed out to them that if they wanted to succeed as retail grocers, they would have to keep their store open on Saturdays—the Jewish Sabbath—they opened a kosher chicken market instead.

As this book goes to press, Moshe and Shmelke's two surviving sisters, Leah and Yitte, are well in their eighties. Leah, whose husband Eli was shot by the Germans, never remarried. She first lived in Newark, but eventually followed most of the family to Elizabeth, New Jersey. Leah's daughter, Feyge Chashe (now known as Fay), the little girl who miraculously survived the dose of poison given to her in Mrs. Halamajowa's hayloft, is now a real estate broker in West Orange, New Jersey. Fay's husband, Milton Malkin, is an attorney. Fay has a daughter, Debra, who graduated from New York University's School of Advertising. Debra was married to Kevin Schweitzer in April 1993.

Yitte is married to Zalman Nachfolger, a *shochet* (ritual slaughterer) whom she met at Randshofen. The couple live in the Boro Park section of Brooklyn, New York, a neighborhood of strictly Or-

(Left to right) Yitte, Moshe, Lea and Schmelke.—May, 1992

*The Nachfolger family.
Front row: Shmuel Moshe
and Liba. Seated, second
row: Shlomo Joseph, his
wife Tsirel with Mendel
on her lap. Standing:
Rivka Dvora, Sruli and
Etty Fala. Standing, rear:
Alter Dovid.*

thodox Jews. Their son, Shlomo Joseph (Yoshie), a chemist, attended Yeshiva Rabbi Chaim Berlin for his Talmudic studies. Yoshie lives with his wife, Tzirel, and their seven children in Monsey, New York.

Shmelke Maltz, now known to the younger generation as Sam (Sam Suchman died many years ago) is in his late seventies. Since his retirement in 1976, he has lived in Elizabeth, He is married to Anna (Hanka) Zielonedrzewo, who he met at night school in Newark, Hanka's father, Abraham Yeshayahu, was a musician. Hanka, who was born in Sosnowice, Poland, was 16 years old when World War II broke out. She lost her entire family in the Holocaust. She herself survived five concentration camps. Shmelke and Hanka have one daughter, Miriam Rivke. A graduate of Yeshiva University's Stern College for Women, Miriam Rivke lives near her parents in Elizabeth with her husband, Philip Schiffman, an accountant. The Schiffmans have two daughters and one son: Rachel Esther Dvora, Leah Chaya Tzirel and Avraham Yeshayahu Meir (Avi).

Chaim (known in the family as Herb), in his mid-fifties, still has clear recollections of the Sokal ghetto and Mrs. Halamajowa's hayloft. He graduated from Rutgers College of Pharmacy in 1958. His brother, Joseph Nathan, a 1969 graduate of the Rutgers Pharmacy College, established a pharmacy in Brooklyn. Herbert and he now own a pharmacy, home health care and surgical supply house.

In 1960, Herbert married Jacqueline Katz. They have four children

Chaim and family. (Bottom row, L to R) Seated: Lisa holding Gavriel,
Rifka Reena holding Elimeir, Jackie with Nechama, Chaim (Herb) holding
Moshe who was named after the author, Dvora holding Sara.
(Standing L to R) Benjy Averick, Dr. Michael Maltz, Amit Schejter and Judy,
Rabbi Steven Hirschey.

Dedication of presenting a medal to Mrs. Halamajowa on being a righteous
gentile, at the Israel Consulate office in New York, 1986. (Seated L to R) Fay,
Yitta. (Standing L to R) Schmelke, Chana, Lea. (Rear row, L to R) Mrs.
Halammajowa's three grandchildren who received the medal for their
grandmother., Chaim and Moshe, the author of this book.

and five grandchildren. Their eldest child, Judith, born in 1961, is now living in Israel. An economics graduate of Barnard College, she was formerly a financial writer for *The Jerusalem Post* and now writes for the Israeli daily *HaAretz* and the *Financial Times* of London. In 1993, Judith married Amit Schejter, a lawyer from Ramat Hasharon. Judy and Amit live in Jerusalem.

The second child (and only son), Mordechai Aryeh, informally known as Michael, born in 1963, graduated from Yeshiva University and the New Jersey College of Medicine and Dentistry. In 1990 he married Rivka Reena Hochbaum of New York City. They have a son, Eliezer Meir. Michael is presently practicing periodontics in New City, New York.

The third child of Herbert and Jacqueline Maltz, Lisa, born in 1966, lives in Chicago. A graduate of the Columbia University School of Engineering, Lisa is married to Benjamin Averick, an accountant. They have one daughter Nechama, and two sons, Gavriel Reuven and Moshe (named after his great-grandfather, Moshe Maltz).

The fourth and youngest child of the Herbert Maltzes, Dvora, was born in 1970. She is named for her great-aunt Chaye Dvora, who died in Mrs. Halamajowa's hayloft. She is a graduate of Yeshiva University's Sy Syms School of Business. Dvora is married to Rabbi Steven Hirshey. They have a daughter, Sara Meira.

Moshe Maltz's second son, Joseph Nathan, lives in Boro Park, Brooklyn. He is married to Tzirel Lemmer.

Joseph Nathan and Tzirel Maltz have three sons and three daughters. The eldest, Meir Zvi, now 20, is studying pharmacy at Brooklyn College; Menachem, 19, is a college student; Abraham 16, attends a yeshiva high school. The two elder daughters, Goldie, 12, and Rivkah, 10 (the latter named for her father's grandmother Rivkah Suchman Maltz), are studying at a Bais Yaakov school for girls in Brooklyn. The youngest, Miriam Esther, is four years old.

Eli Kindler, after the liberation.

Of the group of 12 that survived the war in Mrs. Halamajowa's hayloft, only four settled in Israel: Dr. David Kindler, his wife, Clara, and their two sons, Simcha (Sever) and Eli. They eventually settled in the garden city of Ramat

Nathan (Yosef Nathan) and family: Goldie, Avrumie, Tzirel (Nathan's wife), Rifka, Nathan, Menachem and Meir Zvi is holding Miriam.

Sam (Schmelke) Maltz and family: (Front row, L to R) Rachel and Leah. (Middle row) Daughter Miriam Ryfka holding Avi, Mrs. Maltz, Mr. Sam (Schmelke) Maltz. (Standing in rear) Miriam's husband Phillip.

Gan. Dr. Kindler joined the staff of the Hebrew University–Hadassah Medical Center at En HaKerem near Jerusalem. Dr. Kindler died sometime in the 1980s at the age of 93. Simcha, who lives in the city of Holon, is chief electrician at the plant of the newspaper *Ma'ariv*. Eli, who lives in Ramat Gan, is a computer programmer for Histadrut, Israel's general federation of labor.

Franciska Halamajowa and her daughter Hela are long dead, but Hela's three children, Thaddeusz Linyewski, Yalanta Staran and Graszyna Kocharzyk, are still living. Thaddeusz is in Poland where he is working for a frozen food processing plant. His two sisters are married and live in Hartford, Connecticut.

On January 13, 1986, Franciska Halamajowa's three grandchildren helped honor their grandmother's memory at a reception given at the Israeli Consulate General in New York City. While three generations of Maltzes looked on, Consul General Moshe Yegar handed to Mrs. Halamajowa's grandchildren a certificate and a silver medallion from Yad Vashem, the Heroes' and Martyrs' Remembrance Authority in Jerusalem. Engraved on the medallion was Mrs. Halamajowa's name, encircled by a passage from the Talmud: "Whoever saves even one life should be regarded as if he had saved the whole world."

At the wedding of Judy and Amit on May 31, 1993. (Seated L to R) Eli Kindler, Simcha's wife, Simcha Kindler and Eli's Wife. (Standing) Chaim (Herb) with daughter Judy.

The author and his wife celebrating   Chaim (Herby Maltz) serving in the
their 50th wedding anniversary   U.S. Army at Fort Sam Houston,
Texas, November, 1959

Chaim (Herbert) and Jackie Maltz.

The original edition was written in 1991–92 and published in 1993. This second edition appears in 1998 with the following updates:

Yitta, Moshe's sister, had the good fortune to attend the weddings of three grandchildren, and recently became a great-grandmother.

Chaim's eldest daughter, Judith, now has two children, a son, Matan, age 4, and a daughter, Tamar Chana, age 2. Judy and her husband, Dr. Amit Schejter, are moving to Zichron Yaacov in Israel.

Chaim's son Michael and his wife Rivka Reena live in Monsey, N.Y., with their son Eliezer Meir, age 7, and daughters Ahuva (Lifsha), age 4, and Dahlia, age 2.

Chaim's daughter Lisa and family in Chicago have a fourth child, Yehuda Leib, 2 years old.

Chaim's youngest daughter, Dvora and her husband, Rabbi Steven Hirschey, have three daughters: Sara Meira, age 6, Chana Brucha (named alter Chaim's mother), age 4, and Dena Shulamit, age 1 1/2.

Moshe Maltz's second son is Joseph Nathan. Nathan's oldest son, Mayer Zvi, married Fraidy Neiman in 1997; his second son, Menachem, married Chani Ackerman in 1996. Nathan's sons and their wives are all registered pharmacists. Both families live in Brooklyn, N.Y.

Chaim's daughter Dvora and her family. (From left) Sara, age 5 1/2, Rabbi Steven Hirschey holding Dena, age 1, Dvora, Chana, age 3 1/2.

Chaim's daughter Lisa and her family. (Top) Benjy Averick, Yehuda Leib, age 2, Lisa. (Bottom) Nechama, age 8, Gavriel, age 6 1/2. Moshe (named after the author), age 5.

...hmelke's daughter Miriam and her family. (Top, from left) Lea, age 13, Phillip, Mir-...m. (Bottom, from left) Rachel, age 15, Avi, age 8

Hanka and Shmelke, 1998

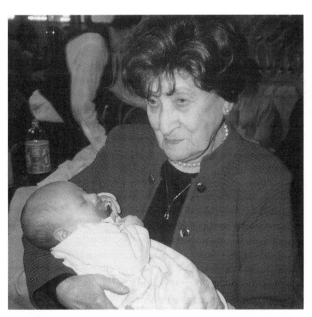

Yitta with her first great-grandchild, Yitzchak Rafael.

Nathan and family. (Standing L to R) Menachem, Tzirel (Nathan's wife), Fraidy and Mayer, Nathan, Avrumie. (Seated L to R) Rivka, Chani (Menachem's wife), Mrs. Lemmer (Nathan's mother-in-law), Goldie. On the floor: Miriam Esther

Chaim's daughter Judith and her family. Judy, Dr. Amit Schejter, Matan Gavriel, age 4, and Tamar Chana, age 2.

Chaim's son Michael and his family. (L to R) Ahuva (Lifsha), age 4, Dr. Michael, Rivka Reena, Dahlia, age 2, Eliezer Meir, age 7.